The Political Economy of Arms Reduction

Reversing Economic Decay

AAAS Selected Symposia Series

 Published by Westview Press, Inc.
5500 Central Avenue, Boulder, Colorado

for the

 American Association for the Advancement of Science
1776 Massachusetts Avenue, N.W., Washington, D.C.

The Political Economy of Arms Reduction

Reversing Economic Decay

Edited by Lloyd J. Dumas

AAAS Selected Symposium **80**

AAAS Selected Symposia Series

This book is based on a symposium which was held at the 1981 AAAS National
Annual Meeting in Toronto, Ontario, January 3-8. The symposium was sponsored
by the AAAS Council and cosponsored by the AAAS Committee on Science, Engineering, and Public Policy.

Published in 1982 in the United States of America by
    Westview Press, Inc.
    5500 Central Avenue
    Boulder, Colorado 80301
    Frederick A. Praeger, President and Publisher

Library of Congress Catalog Card Number 82-060047
ISBN 0-86531-405-5

Printed and bound in the United States of America

About the Book

     The old and oft-quoted dictum, "If you want peace, pre-
pare for war," may have the appearance of wisdom, but historical evidence to the contrary is overwhelming--preparation for
war leads to war. If we are to avoid war and establish and
maintain peace, asserts Dr. Dumas, we must prepare for peace.
The legacy of 35 years of the post-World War II arms race has
been reduced security and economic decay for all participants.
Arms reduction has thus become a key component of economic
revitalization and security improvement. One important part of
this preparation, he continues, must be plans for the smooth
and effective transfer of productive resources from military
to civilian-oriented activities.

     This volume focuses on the economic damage caused by
arms expenditures and analyzes the nature of and solutions to
the problems of transition in both the U.S. and the USSR. The
role of the military in industrial technology is explored. The
particular stake of the labor force in this transition is discussed by the president of one of the largest unions representing defense workers in the U.S., and is further amplified by
analysis of the organized labor campaign to transfer production to "socially useful" products at Europe's largest aerospace firm. Finally, a model for institutionalizing decentralized contingency planning for this transition in the U.S.
is discussed.

About the Series

The *AAAS Selected Symposia Series* was begun in 1977 to provide a means for more permanently recording and more widely disseminating some of the valuable material which is discussed at the AAAS Annual National Meetings. The volumes in this *Series* are based on symposia held at the Meetings which address topics of current and continuing significance, both within and among the sciences, and in the areas in which science and technology impact on public policy. The *Series* format is designed to provide for rapid dissemination of information, so the papers are not typeset but are reproduced directly from the camera-copy submitted by the authors. The papers are organized and edited by the symposium arrangers who then become the editors of the various volumes. Most papers published in this *Series* are original contributions which have not been previously published, although in some cases additional papers from other sources have been added by an editor to provide a more comprehensive view of a particular topic. Symposia may be reports of new research or reviews of established work, particularly work of an interdisciplinary nature, since the AAAS Annual Meetings typically embrace the full range of the sciences and their societal implications.

WILLIAM D. CAREY
Executive Officer
American Association for
the Advancement of Science

Contents

vii

About the Editor and Authors

Lloyd J. Dumas *is associate professor of political economy at the University of Texas, Dallas. He has written on the impact of military expenditures on the domestic economy and on disarmament and economy in the U.S. and USSR. He is a member of the AAAS Committee on Science, Arms Control and National Security.*

Kenneth E. Boulding *is distinguished professor of economics emeritus and research associate/project director at the Institute of Behavioral Science, University of Colorado, Boulder. Among his many books are* Stable Peace *(University of Texas Press, 1978),* Kenneth Boulding/Collected Papers, vol. V: International Systems: Peace, Conflict Resolution, and Politics *(ed. by L. D. Singell; Colorado Associated University Press, 1975), and* Conflict and Defense *(Harper, 1962). He is a former president of the American Association for the Advancement of Science, the American Economic Association, and the International Studies Association.*

Seymour Melman, *professor of industrial engineering and operations research at Columbia University, has specialized in studies of productivity and the problems of conversion from military to civilian industry. He is the author of* The Permanent War Economy: American Capitalism in Decline *(Simon and Schuster, 1974) and* Pentagon Capitalism: The Political Economy of War *(McGraw-Hill, 1970), and he edited the six-volume series* Conversion of Industry from a Military to Civilian Economy *(Praeger, 1970).*

David F. Noble, *a specialist in the history of technology, is an associate professor in the Program in Science, Technology, and Society at Massachusetts Institute of Technology. He is the author of* America by Design: Science, Technology, and the Rise of Corporate Capitalism *and* Forces of Production *(Knopf, 1977 and 1982, respectively).*

William Winpisinger, *currently international president of the International Association of Machinists and Aerospace Workers, has been active in union organizing for more than thirty years. He is a member of the Executive Council of the AFL-CIO and the Economic Committee of the American Association for the United Nations. He is co-chair of the National Planning Association Board, the Democratic Socialist Organizing Committee, and of SANE, a citizen's group involved with nuclear weapons and arms race policy issues.*

The Lucas Aerospace Combine Shop Stewards Committee, *representing workers from 17 worksites and 13 trade unions, was formed in 1970 to combat massive worker layoffs and factory closures in Great Britain. Relying on information provided by Lucas engineers and workers, the committee developed an alternate corporate plan designed to change production from military-related to socially useful products.*

Foreword

Just as excuses seem to move people to action much more than reasons, legends, especially when they contain half-truths, seem to have a larger niche in the ecosystem of the human mind than does history. Perhaps, therefore, it is one of the great tasks of the human intellect to find excuses for things which are reasonable to do so that people will do them and so create history which is both true and has the power of legend. This volume is an important contribution to this intellectual task, especially to the latter one.

There is a very powerful legend in the American consciousness, that only Hitler got us out of the Great Depression, and that, therefore, we need a large war industry to prevent depression. The legend about Hitler is at least a half-truth. We had gotten halfway out of the Great Depression by 1937, by the sheer spontaneous revival of gross private domestic investment and the rise in profits above interest which resulted. We did have a relapse in 1938, thanks largely to the introduction of Social Security and the large cash surplus which resulted in the first year, when it was virtually all contributions and practically no benefits. After 1938-1939 it is undoubtedly true that the rise of the war industry, which was something under 1.0 percent of the GNP in the early thirties and 42 percent in 1944, virtually eliminated unemployment, though it almost destroyed local government, which took 20 years to recover and, of course, quite severely restricted consumption.

The history which somehow never became legend is that of the great disarmament, when in one year, 1945-46, we transferred 30 percent of the GNP from the war industry into civilian uses, without unemployment ever rising above 3 percent, an astonishing testimony to the flexibility of the American economy and also to some wise planning by the Committee for Economic Development at the local level. For some reason this never became a legend in the American mind. Hardly any-body knows it. So the fiction that the war industry is neces-sary for full employment took firm hold on the American public.

This volume does not deal with the question as to wheth-er the war industry in fact defends us, about which there is grave doubt. But whether it does or not, these papers clear-ly bring out the cost of the war industry, which is very high. It has averaged somewhere between 7 and 8 percent since the end of the Korean War, but its qualitative impact has been much larger than this. If we had put that 8 percent into in-vestment, of course, we would be much better off today, and we would certainly all be much richer. Beyond the quantita-tive impact, however, is a much larger qualitative impact. The war industry can quite properly be described as an "eco-nomic cancer" within the American economy, not only because it sucks resources into it, but because its spillover into the American economy is so largely perverse. The fact, for in-stance, that the nuclear power industry is a by-product of the war industry led us into the light-water reactor, which is almost certainly more dangerous and less efficient than possible alternatives. The brain drain into the war industry has deprived us of scientists, engineers, who could have been improving our civilian productivity. Furthermore, the atmos-phere of economic waste, which inevitably pervades a war in-dustry, spreads out far beyond it in attitudes in the indus-trial community.

There is no doubt that the war industry has contributed to make the United States a technological laggard compared with West Germany and Japan, which have not had to pay this economic cost. At the present time, the proposed expansion of the war industry, in a mildly sick economy, is almost certain to produce further acceleration in inflation. Israel, with 25 percent of its economy in the war industry, now more than doubles its price level every year, and we may well be getting into the same boat.

There are no easy answers to these questions, but the worst possible answer is to pretend that they do not exist. This volume should arouse the public from the complacency it seems to feel on this issue, and the questions that it raises should be in the forefront of economic and political discus-sion. Professor Dumas and his colleagues are much to be con-gratulated on a volume of great timeliness and significance.

Kenneth E. Boulding
University of Colorado,
Boulder

1. Military Spending and Economic Decay

Introduction

The terrible social and economic trauma of the Great
Depression and the prolonged boom during and after the Second
World War that finally laid it to rest, deeply imbedded an
economic lesson in the American psyche: military spending
stimulates production, creates employment and generally
brings prosperity. The problem with this well-learned lesson
is that it is based on a combination of shoddy empiricism
and poor economics, and more importantly, it is absolutely
untrue.

Ultimately, the degree of material well-being generated
by any economy depends not only on its ability to fully
employ the productive resources (labor, capital, materials,
energy, etc.) available to it, but also on its ability to
employ them in ways that contribute to the societal standard
of living. The production of ordinary consumer goods and
services, such as food, clothing, housecleaning, barbering,
etc. clearly add directly to the present material living
standard. The production of producer goods and associated
services, such as industrial machinery, rail transportation
systems, factory buildings, supporting engineering consulting
services, etc. is also contributive, but through a less
direct route. This class of goods and services expands an
economy's ability to produce, and by so doing enhances the
supply of consumer-oriented output in the future. Hence it
contributes not to the present, but to the future standard
of living. There are also categories of mixed goods, i.e.,
both consumer and producer goods combined, the most prominent
examples of which are probably education and health care.
Resource use for the supply of mixed goods as well must
therefore be considered productive since they augment both
the present and the future standard of living.

Military oriented production however falls into a wholly different category. It does not add to the supply of consumer goods or to the supply of producer goods, and so contributes to neither the present nor future material standard of living. Resources put to this use can then be said to have been diverted, i.e., channeled away from ordinary contributive use. They are not, in and of themselves, adding to material well-being.

When resources which have been idle are put to work, whether or not that work is useful, unemployment will be reduced, income will be distributed and at least the short-run appearance of prosperity will be achieved. But if those resources have been used unproductively, they will in the long term be a drain on the society. Because resources are being wasted, things which need doing will not be done, and so the economy and the wider society will suffer.

The issue of the use to which resources are put is so fundamental and so overriding in its impact on the ability of an economy to efficiently generate economically useful goods and services that economic systems as distinct as those of capitalism and communism experience similar structural problems when resources are diverted from contributive use. This is particularly true over the long run.

During the half decade or so of heavy World War II military spending in the U.S., neglect of the renewal of various types of civilian oriented equipment and facilities (e.g. railroads, mass transit systems, industrial equipment), and neglect of civilian oriented technological development did not create major problems. Such capital equipment is long-lived, and sizeable technological leads do not typically disappear quickly. But as the substantial diversion of productive resources stretched from half a decade to three decades, severe strains and stresses did occur. And we see the effects of this sapping of our economic vitality all around us.

Neither capitalist nor socialist economies are capable of overriding negative economic effects of persistently high military spending. Differences in economic systems and circumstance, however, can and do influence the way in which the economic distress surfaces.

As will be discussed, the economic damage done by the military burden in the U.S. has surfaced mainly in the form of simultaneously high inflation and high unemployment, through the intervening variable of deteriorating produc-

tivity. In contrast, in the U.S.S.R., the damage has
surfaced mainly in the form of chronic problems of supplying
sufficient quantity and quality of goods and services--
particularly consumer goods and services. There are two main
reasons for these differences.

First, the military economy of the U.S. developed, post
World War II, alongside a well developed and booming civilian
economy. In fact, the U.S. was the only major industrial
nation in the world not devastated by the horrors of that
war. The Soviet military economy, on the other hand, developed alongside a civilian economy massively damaged by that
conflict and itself struggling hard to develop. Thus, the
Soviet civilian economy was never able to work on breaking
its chronic supply problems with a major, systematic and
sustained effort. On the contrary, shortages were continually made more severe by the demands of the military economy
under the impetus of an escalating superpower arms race.

Second, the differences between the capitalist and
communist economic systems make it easier for the latter to
prevent unemployment and cope with inflation. A capitalist
economy must rely on the voluntary actions of individuals
seeking private economic gain (in present forms, with more
or less government intervention) in order to provide employment, while relying on such private decisions, along with
the impersonal mechanism of competition and governmental
control of the money supply to control inflation; a communist economy, on the other hand, features direct government
control of both employment opportunities and prices (though
the latter tends to be somewhat more subject to external
influence through rising import costs). On the other hand,
incentive problems, along with ponderous bureaucratic and
informational difficulties, tend to make adequate supply and
coordination of supply with demand more difficult for a
communist economy than for one operated by capitalist
principles.

But doesn't the military contribute to the standard of
living by protecting the nation and its people, i.e., by
providing the consumption good "security"? Does it not
therefore constitute a contributive resource use?

In the first place, the definition of "security" as a
consumer good to be lumped in with all other consumer goods
is yet another example of the tendency of economists to end
run around sticky analytic problems by definitional manipulation, not unlike defining goods of differing quality to be
different goods in order to avoid facing the difficult

issues of quality measurement and competition. Security is, of course, necessary, but its production does not contribute to the material standard of living in quite the same way as does the production of cars, TV's, furniture, housing, machine tools, trucks, etc. It is, in a sense, a "necessary evil" type of activity, and as such is most usefully viewed as burden on the directly and indirectly contributive elements of the economy. And since it is an economically painful activity, common sense would indicate that it needs to be constantly scrutinized and reviewed with an eye toward keeping it as small as possible, consistent with real security needs.

Secondly, it is not difficult to demonstrate that the stockpiling and expansion of military forces is an extremely costly and inefficient means of generating "security" at best. The lengthy U.S. experience in the Vietnam War, the ineffectiveness of military force or threat of force in countering the vast international redistribution of income and economic power from the industrialized world to the nations of OPEC, the inability of the extremely well-financed and well-supplied army of the Shah of Iran to prevail over an aroused population armed with "sticks and stones"--all of these and more should have by now taught us something about the limits of military power in protect-ing security interests (rightly or wrongly perceived) abroad. Furthermore, it is an undeniable fact of the nuclear age that there is not a thing the U.S. or Soviet militaries can do to protect their countries against being turned into smoldering radioactive wastelands within a couple of hours if either launches an all out nuclear attack against the other. Is this security?

Finally, as I have argued in some detail elsewhere, the nuclear and associated forces beyond those necessary to constitute a minimal deterrent are not merely useless, but for military and technical reasons tend to substantially degrade security.[1] This is chiefly due to reliability problems interacting with excessive weaponry and associated systems to exacerbate problems of nuclear weapons accidents, accidental war, theft of weapons by hostile forces (includ-ing terrorists) and so on. Incorporating these effects into a theoretical arms race model centered on the desire of participants to maximize security further elaborates the security reducing character of an interactive arms race.[2] This view is corroborated by the observation and arguments of such participants in the dynamics of the real world arms race as Herbert F. York, former Director of Defense Research and Engineering in the Department of Defense, and of Liver-more Laboratories.[3]

But the main focus of this present analysis is not on
the issue of security per se, but rather on the particular
economic effects of military expenditure. And it is that
question to which attention is now directed.

The fullest explication of these effects will be in the
U.S. context, not because the damage is greater there or more
easily understood, but simply because the relative availability of data and analysis is presently so much greater than
for the U.S.S.R. Some of the analysis, however, is fairly
easily translatable into the Soviet situation.

There are essentially four reasons why the maintenance
of high levels of military expenditure in the U.S. during the
post-World War II period has massively contributed to the
generation of both inflation and unemployment. These are:
(1) the economic nature of military goods; (2) the way in
which military procurement has been conducted; (3) effects on
the international balance of payments; and (4) effects on
civilian technological progress. Each of these is now
considered in turn.

The Economic Nature of Military Goods

Military goods are those products purchased by the military which are to some degree specialized to military use.
Thus, tanks, rifles, bombs, fighter planes, etc. are military
goods, while milk, meat, detergents, etc. purchased by the
armed forces are not.

Despite the fact that military goods do not produce
economic value in the sense of contribution to the material
standard of living, as has been discussed, they do require
valuable economic resources for their production, and therefore impose a real cost on society. This cost is best
measured not purely in terms of money, but rather in terms of
the sacrifice of the economically and socially useful goods
and services that could have been produced with the labor,
materials, energy, machinery, etc. which were instead devoted
to military production.

Now, the money that flows to producers of military goods
in exchange for their products is spent by the firms primarily
on producer goods and by their workforces primarily on consumer goods. Thus these funds injected into the economy by
the government call forth increased demand for consumer and
producer goods without a corresponding increase in supply of
either consumer or producer goods. The excess demand that
tends to result, or put simply the situation of too many
dollars chasing after too few goods, is a classic economic

prescription for inflation. For example, during nearly all
of the latter part of the decade of the 1960's, when the U.S.
involvement in the Vietnam War was intensifying, the unemployment rate was under 4%.[4] Military spending was not offset, and between 1965 and 1969, the rate of inflation more
than tripled.[5]

There were and are clearly no purely economic reasons
for failing to offset expansions in military spending with
higher taxation. Nor can this failure be explained by
ignorance of the probably inflationary effects of failing to
do so, since existing well accepted macroeconomic theory
would predict this part of the inflationary effect. Rather,
this policy (or lack thereof) seems more readily attributable
to a political calculation that raising taxes for the express
purpose of supporting increased military activity might have
quickened and heightened public opposition, particularly
during Vietnam, since the economic costs of this activity
would be made more explicit. So a political sleight-of-hand
approach was adopted, making the public pay through increased
inflation that eroded their purchasing power, rather than
through direct taxation. It was a strategy that relied upon
the unlikelihood that the public would directly connect the
war and subsequent military expansion with the growing inflation about which they grew more and more concerned. And
by all appearances, this strategy has been and still appears
to be politically effective.

Military Procurement Practices

Care has been taken, over the years, to develop a
variety of payment formulas for military contracts to provide
strong incentives for military industrial firms to produce
efficiently, that is to produce products meeting the agreed
upon performance specifications, adhere to agreed delivery
schedules and hold costs down to a minimum. However, none
of these payment formulas work. In practice, whatever the
formulas formally written into major military procurement
contracts, the contracts are effectively performed on a "cost
plus" basis.[6]

A detailed analysis of this problem seems inappropriate
here, but in essence there appear to be two main reasons why
this is so. One seems to be in the fact that the formulas
are designed to provide appropriate incentives for efficiency
on the assumption that the firm involved is interested in
maximizing profits. The incentives collapse to an essentially cost-plus situation in the case of a sales maximizing
firm. The other reason seems to be a plain and simple
failure of the government to enforce the terms of the

contract, an explanation that admittedly raises more questions than it answers.[7]

In any case, operating under an effectively cost-plus
system, the producing firm is paid an amount equal to its
total cost of production (whatever that eventually turns out
to be) plus a guaranteed profit. Thus, the firm involved not
only has no risk, but also has no incentive to hold its costs
down. In fact, to the extent that the firm wants to increase
its sales revenue, it will have a very powerful incentive to
run its costs up in order to achieve the highest possible
payment for its product.

Combining this incentive system with the very large
amounts of money made available for military procurement year
after year by the Congress has created a situation in which
military industry can and does pay whatever is necessary and
then some for whatever resources it needs or wants. As a
result, it has bid up the price of those resources--resources
like machine tools, engineers and scientists, skilled machinists, etc. To the extent that other industries require these
same resources, they now face increased costs and hence feel
pressed to raise their prices. Thus a cost-push inflationary pressure is fed throughout not only the military sector,
but the entire economy.

Aside from its direct inflationary effects on resource
costs, the purchasing power of defense firms, backed by
their rich customer (the Federal Government), has completely
pre-empted a substantial amount of some of these resources,
with serious long-term effects on the health of the civilian
economy.

For example, by crude and conservative estimate nearly
one-third of all the engineers and scientists in the United
States were engaged in defense-related work (discussed
below). This can be taken as a lower limit on the true
figure. It seems more likely that the figure is higher,
perhaps as high as one-half. Whether the actual figure is
one-third or one-half, the crucial point is that a great
deal of the nation's technological talent has been diverted
to the development of military and military-related technology. The pre-emption by the military of such a large
fraction of what we will subsequently see is a critical resource in a modern industrial society, cannot fail to have
significant effects on the functioning of that part of the
economy that produces goods and services which, unlike military goods, do contribute to the standard of living and the
quality of life. Furthermore, it is important to understand
that this magnitude or pre-emption of technological resources

Table 1.   U.S. military expenditures abroad and the international balance of payments.

Year[1]	Balance of Trade[2] ($millions)	Balance of Payments[3] ($millions)	Net Direct Defense Expenditures Abroad[4] ($millions)
1955	2,897	--	2,501
1956	4,753	--	2,627
1957	6,271	--	2,466
1958	3,462	--	2,835
1959	1,148	--	2,503
1960	4,892	-3,667	2,752
1961	5,571	-2,252	2,596
1962	4,521	-2,864	2,449
1963	5,224	-2,713	2,304
1964	6,801	-2,696	2,133
1965	4,951	-2,478	2,122
1966	3,817	-2,151	2,935
1967	3,800	-4,683	3,226
1968	635	-1,611	3,143
1969	607	-6,081	3,328
1970	2,603	-3,851	3,354
1971	-2,268	-21,965	2,893
1972	-6,409	-13,829	3,621
1973	955	-7,651	2,316
1974	-5,528	-19,043	2,159
TOTAL	48,703		54,263

Notes: 1. Problems of data availability and comparability
            complicate a more complete analysis over the
            entire post World War II period.
         2. Exports-imports, merchandise, adjusted excluding
            military (minus implies deficit).
         3. Net liquidity balance (minus implies deficit).
         4. Direct defense expenditures - military sales
            (does not include military grants of goods and
            services).

Sources: Bureau of Economic Analysis, U.S. Department of
           Commerce, Business Statistics (1973), pp. 13-14,
           and Survey of Current Business (June 1975),
           pp. 26, 30.

has been maintained for two to three decades or more. But full discussion of the implications of this pre-emption will be deferred for now.

'   Thus directly through its effects on bidding up certain resource costs and less directly though more powerfully by its pre-emption of key resources from the civilian economy, the free spending procurement practices of military industry have contributed importantly to the ongoing inflation.

International Balance of Payments Effects

From 1893 through 1970, year by year the U.S. had a balance of trade surplus, i.e. the U.S. exported a greater value of goods and services than it imported. Since exports bring foreign currency into the U.S., while imports send U.S. dollars abroad, if this had been the only aspect of the U.S. international transactions, there would have been a considerable accumulation of foreign currencies (or gold) in the U.S., and comparative shortage of U.S. dollars abroad. Consequently, by 1971 the U.S. dollar would have been one of the strongest (if not the strongest) currencies in the world. Instead, in 1971 the U.S. dollar was officially devalued, in formal recognition of its declining worth relative to key foreign currencies. How could this seeming paradox occur?

The balance of payments, the total net figure of international currency flows includes not only money flows related to trade, but all other international money flows as well (e.g. foreign investments in the U.S., profits flowing from U.S. subsidiaries abroad into the U.S., foreign aid, etc.). And the U.S. balance of payments has been in continuous deficit for decades now.

What role has U.S. military expenditure played in this situation? It has affected the U.S. international economic position directly through outflows of dollars for defense expenditures abroad, and indirectly through its effects on the balance of trade, chiefly via its influence on the competitiveness of U.S. civilian industries in domestic and foreign markets. This latter effect is extremely important and will be discussed in detail subsequently.

Table 1 presents some basic U.S. Department of Commerce data which bear on the direct effects of military expenditures abroad and on the U.S. international financial situation. We note that the entire cumulative balance of payments deficit for the period 1960-1970 (inclusive) was $35 billion, whereas over the same period, total direct defense expenditures (net after military sales abroad) were more than $30 billion. Hence, U.S. military expenditures abroad accounted for 86.6% of the entire U.S. balance of payments deficit during that period.

During the years 1966-1970 (inclusive) there was a huge inflow of foreign currencies into the U.S., represented by a cumulative balance of trade surplus of nearly $62 billion. But during those same years, net military expenditures abroad were responsible for an outflow of dollars from the U.S. amounting to more than $43 billion. The outflow of U.S. currency owing to military spending abroad thus wiped out 69.9% of the balance of trade surplus, 1955-1970.

These comparisons greatly understate the magnitude of U.S. defense expenditures abroad, because they do not include outright U.S. grants of military goods and services. Since they involve no international flows of currency, these gifts of military equipment and services are not involved in the balance of money flows. However, if included, the total of almost $34 billion worth of such grants recorded during the years 1960-1974 would increase the military expenditure figures given for that period by more than 80%.

It is clear from these data that direct outflows of dollars in the form of U.S. military expenditures abroad played a major role in destroying the favorable balance of trade surplus, and contributed to the severe weakening of the U.S. dollar. This substantially raised the price of imported goods (including oil) upon which the nation's business and consumers have become increasingly dependent in the past few years. Even when an imported product has not had a price increase in terms of its native currency, the declining value of the dollar relative to that currency will result in a rising dollar price. Insofar as consumer goods are directly imported then from countries against whose currency the dollar is weakening, this will contribute straight-forwardly to domestic inflation. When industrial goods and resources are imported the effect of a failing dollar in raising their prices will result in a broad cost-push pressure on all U.S. industries using these goods and resources (and there are many, many such industries). To the extent that this pressure cannot be offset (a phenomenon that will be discussed shortly), rising prices of these domestically produced goods will result, further exacerbating inflation. Thus, the massive outflow of military spending abroad has directly and substantially contributed to the generation of inflation within the domestic U.S. economy.

But what of the huge increases in international oil prices in recent years? Has this, rather than the military, not been the major cause of the international weakening of the dollar and its corresponding inflationary effects?

A simple look at the sequence of events is sufficient
to demonstrate that neither the international breaking of
the value of the dollar nor the high inflation/high unemployment economy of the U.S. could have been initiated by
the actions of the Organization of Petroleum Exporting
Countries (OPEC). In the first place, the U.S. has been
suffering from unprecedented simultaneous high inflation/
high unemployment every year since 1969. Secondly, the
dollar was officially devalued for the first time in modern
U.S. history in 1971. But the OPEC oil embargo and the subsequent huge increases in oil prices did not even occur
until late 1973!

That is not to say that the OPEC oil price escalation
has not contributed significantly to the piling up of
dollars abroad and to the U.S. general economic woes.
Certainly, it has had an important exacerbating effect,
particularly in conjunction with the progressive loss of
cost offsetting capability by U.S. industries, a phenomenon
clearly and importantly related to the military drain on the
nation's civilian economy (as will be discussed in detail).
But the chronology makes it obvious that it could not have
been the fundamental cause of these problems.

Impact of Military Spending on Civilian Technology
and the Implications Thereof

Allocation of scientific and engineering resources to
military-oriented activity. Since the beginning of the
Second World War and with substantially more force since the
latter half of the 1950's, the United States has channeled a
large fraction of the nation's engineering and scientific
resources into military-related research. Some of this has
been direct, through priority allocation of Federal Government grants for these purposes; and some has been indirect,
through the utilization of a considerable portion of the
annual discretionary federal budget for purchase of increasingly technologically sophisticated weapons and related
systems whose research, development and production required
military industrial firms to hire large quantities of
technologists.

According to National Science Foundation (NSF) data,
over the entire decade of the 1970's, the fraction of yearly
Federal budget obligations for research and development going
to the military and space programs averaged more than two-
thirds of the total. More than half of this money was
channeled to the military alone.[8] Looked at from another
angle, as of the mid-1970's, 77% of the nation's research
and development engineers and scientists (excluding social
scientists) who received Federal support, received it from

the Department of Defense (DoD), National Aeronautics and
Space Administration (NASA) and the Atomic Energy Commission
(AEC)--again more than 50% from the DoD alone.[9] Nearly
three-quarters of the engineers and scientists employed by
business and industry who received federal support in that
year received it from the same three agencies.[10]

Estimation of the fraction of the nation's total engineering and scientific talent engaged in military-related
research is quite a bit more tortuous a task than it should
be, primarily because publicly available data are not categorized in such a manner as to expedite this effort. For
instance, published NSF data on characteristics of the
nation's engineering and scientific employment for 1974 contains a table entitled, "Number of Scientists and Engineers
by Field, Highest Degree and Critical National Interest."[11]

Though some ten categories of "critical national interest" are listed, ranging from "health," "food," "housing,"
etc. to "space," military work or its standard euphemism
"national defense" is not one of them. Apparently, the NSF
does not consider national defense a "critical national
interest." Not surprisingly, the two miscellaneous categories in the table, labelled "does not apply" and "no
report," which must therefore contain the bulk of the military-related engineers and scientists, constitute more than
57% of the total.

While the making of an accurate, up-to-date estimate of
the military sector pre-emption of scientific and engineering talent, given this obfuscation, would be an involved and
arduous task without access to primary data, it is possible
to produce reasonable and fairly conservative rough estimates by manipulating some of the published data for the mid-
1970's (most recent, at this writing). For example, if one
assumes that only half of the engineers and scientists falling into the two miscellaneous categories of the NSF's
"critical national interest" table just discussed are engaged in military work (n.b. ten major categories of national interest have already been explicitly subtracted), an
estimate just under 30% of the total national pool of engineers and scientists results, whether the calculation is
done with or without social scientists, and whether or not
personnel with less than a bachelor's degree are included.
Adding in the numbers explicitly listed for "space" research, raises the fraction to just above 33%.

The estimate can be approached from another angle by
extracting the numbers of full-time equivalent R & D
scientists and engineers for three major military-oriented

industry categories "electrical equipment and communication," "aircraft and missiles" and "machinery" from NSF data for 1967.[12] Assuming that roughly two-thirds of the R & D engineers and scientists in the first two industries and only one-quarter of those in the third industry are engaged in military-related work, and ignoring all other industries completely (industries ignored would include tank production, ordinance, nuclear submarines, etc.) results in an estimate of just under 33% for military-oriented engineering and scientific industrial R & D employment.

Though it is inappropriate to rely heavily on the accuracy of estimates so crudely developed, it would appear likely that an important fraction of the engineering and scientific personnel in the U.S. have been devoting their talents to the development of military-oriented technology, and unlikely that the fraction would be substantially less than one-third. In all probability, it is far higher. And in any case, it is important to remember that this magnitude of pre-emption of technological resources has been maintained for two to three decades or more.

Impact on civilian-oriented technological development. The kind of new technological knowledge that will ultimately emerge from any given research or development project will, of course, not be wholly predictable in advance. By definition, the researchers are engaged in a quest for new knowledge, and such explorations of the unknown and untried must always involve uncertainty and a degree of unpredictability. However, even while not wholly determinate, the kind of new technical knowledge developed is very strongly conditioned by the nature of the problems being studied and the type of solutions being sought. Since one-third or more of the nation's engineers and scientists have been seeking military-oriented solutions to military-oriented problems for the past several decades, it should be no surprise that the development of military technology has proceeded at a rapid pace in the U.S.--or that the development of civilian-oriented technology has become severely retarded here. How could it have been otherwise?

The much vaunted "spinoff" or "spillover" argument that military-oriented technological development produces massive improvements in areas of civilian application and thus does not retard civilian technological progress, makes very little conceptual sense, and more to the point, is massively contradicted by straightforward empirical observation. Of course, some transferability of technical knowledge between military and civilian application would be expected (in both directions), but conceptually it is difficult to see how directing attention to one area of technical research would routinely produce an <u>efficient</u> generation of knowledge pertaining to a completely different area.

On the empirical side, a 1974 report of a committee of the National Academy of Engineering stated:

"With a few exceptions the vast technology developed by Federally funded programs since World War II has not resulted in widespread 'spinoffs' of secondary or additional applications of practical products, processes and services that have made an impact on the nation's economic growth, industrial productivity, employment gains and foreign trade."[13]

The seventh annual report of the National Science Board, governing body of the National Science Foundation (<u>Science Indicators</u>-1974) expressed concern over the serious erosion of the U.S. predominance in science and technology. In several international comparisons the empirical indicators behind this concern were detailed:

"The 'patent balance' of the United States fell by about 30% between 1966 and 1973....the decline was due to an increasing number of U.S. patents awarded to foreign countries and a decline (in 1973) in the number of foreign patents awarded to U.S. citizens. Overall, foreign patenting increased in the United States during the period by over 65%, and by 1973 represented more than 30% of all U.S. patents granted. This suggests that the number of patentable ideas of international merit has been growing at a greater rate in other countries than in the United States."[14]

Further, the report describes the relative production of a total of 492 major innovations by the U.S., the U.K., Japan, West Germany and France over the twenty year period from 1953-1973:

"The U.S. lead...declined steadily from the late 1950's to the mid-1960's, falling from 82 to 55% of the innovations. The slight upturn in later years represents a relative rather than an absolute gain, and results primarily from a decline in the proportion of innovations produced in the United Kingdom, rather than an increase in the number of U.S. innovations."[15]

More recently, the NSF's <u>Science Indicators</u>: 1978 (National Science Board, 1979) points to a continuation of these downtrends, the foreign origin share of total U.S.

patents having increased further from 30% in 1973 to 36% in 1977.[16] Furthermore, this high total share of foreign origin patents is clearly not the result of growing foreign success in only one or two areas. "Foreign patents account for between one-third and one-half of all U.S. patents across a wide spectrum of fields."[17] The NSF goes on to point out:

"U.S. patenting has decreased abroad as well as at home ...From 1966 to 1976, U.S. patenting activity abroad declined almost 30% in ten industrialized countries... The decline in U.S. patenting abroad could be attributable to a number of factors, including...a relative decline in the U.S. inventive activity..."[18]

The relatively poor showing of the U.S. is even more remarkable considering that these data do not specifically exclude military-related technology and hence are biased in favor of the U.S. It is interesting to note that in these comparisons, Japan and West Germany did quite well.

"Since 1963, inventors from West Germany have received the largest number of foreign origin U.S. patents (83,220). In fact, among U.S. foreign-origin patents, West Germany was first in 11 of the 15 major product fields and second in the remaining 4...

"Japan ranks second in the number of total U.S. patents granted to foreign investors between 1963 and 1977 (61,510). Japan has the largest number of foreign patents in three product groups...and is second in an additional five categories...Since 1970, Japan has dramatically increased its patent activity by over 100% in every product field except the two areas in which it already had a large concentration of patents. This finding is significant in that it seems to dispute the widespread belief that Japanese R & D efforts are narrowly focused on specific technologies..."[19]

Not so coincidentally, these two countries averaged about 4.0% (Japan, 1961-1975) and 20.0% (West Germany, 1961-1967) of government R & D expenditures on defense and space, as opposed to a U.S. average of about 70% (1961-1977).[20]

In a conceptually related comparison Michael Boretsky of the U.S. Department of Commerce presents data bearing on the relative civilian equivalent R & D effort (allowing for 10% spinoff from defense and space R & D) of the U.S., six European countries, Canada and Japan in the 1960's.[21] In terms of R & D employment, Japan shows a civilian R & D effort nearly three times as intense as that for the U.S.,

West Germany ranks some 60% higher than the U.S.; in fact,
only Italy and Canada rank lower.

Furthermore, again using absolute numbers of patents
granted as a measure of technological progress, and looking
at the U.S. industrial technological progress, and looking at
the U.S. industrial technology situation overall, the NSF
finds:

"The total number of patents granted annually to U.S.
inventors generally increased from 1960 to the early
1970's but showed a steady decline from 1971 to 1977...
Complex influences on the level of patenting make
analysis of patent data difficult...In the present
case, since patenting has dropped in almost all product fields, the trends seem to indicate a real decline
in the rate of production of inventions by U.S. industry
from 1971 to 1977..."[22]

Recognition of the serious retardation of civilian technological progress is also widespread in the nation's business community. In 1976 (February 26), Business Week ran an
article entitled "The Breakdown of U.S. Innovation," the
introduction of which included the phrase "...from boardroom
to research lab there is a growing sense that something has
happened to U.S. innovation...". Apparently that "sense"
continued to grow, because by July 3, 1978 the story had made
the cover of that journal. The article, entitled "Vanishing
Innovation" began, "A grim mood prevails today among industrial research managers. America's vaunted technological
superiority of the 1950's and 1960's is vanishing...." The
government also clearly recognized that a severe problem
existed, as the Carter Administration ordered a massive, 18
month long, 28-agency domestic policy review of the influence
of the government on industrial innovation.

Given the huge amounts of money and technical personnel
which have indisputably been poured into military-related
research over the past several decades in the U.S., the
severity of the slowdown in civilian technological progress
would not have occurred if the 'spinoff' or 'spillover'
effects had been anything more than marginal. But if the
transferability of invention and innovation was and is actually low, then the decades long diversion of at least a
third of the engineers and scientists in the U.S. to military
related work would predictably have produced precisely the
sort of civilian technological deterioration we have, in
fact, experienced. Under conditions of low transferability
it could not have failed to produce such a result.

  <u>Civilian technological progress and productivity growth</u>.
It is widely recognized that civilian technological progress
is the keystone of productivity improvement and economic
growth. As the National Science Board put it in their 1977
annual report (<u>Science Indicators</u>: 1976),

> "...the contribution of R & D to economic growth and
> productivity is positive, significant and high, and
> that such innovation is an important factor---perhaps
> the most important factor---in the economic growth of
> the United States in this century."

According to Boretsky of the Commerce Department,

> "The most relevant historical evidence suggests that
> American technology reached parity with Europe by 1870
> or thereabout.. and by the end of World War II it had
> become a literal 'wonder' to the rest of the world...
> The present concern is not with the country's technol-
> ogy relevant to defense and the conquest of space which
> occupied the last two decades, but with technology
> relevant to the quality of life in society at large as
> well as more specifically, productivity and commercial
> markets at home and abroad."[23]

  Civilian technological progress is that which is oriented to the development of knowledge leading to improved consumer and producer products and to more efficient ways of
producing. These two aspects, new and better products and
improved production methods are not so distinct as it might
seem, since a major source of increase in productive efficiency is the employment of new machinery and equipment
embodying superior technology.

  Civilian technological progress contributes to the
growth of labor productivity by encouraging increases in the
quantity of capital per worker and to the growth of both
labor and capital productivity through the development of
production techniques enabling the more efficient use of
productive resources in general. Accordingly, as the development of civilian technology became increasingly retarded in
the U.S., productivity growth began to collapse.

  From 1947 to 1975, output per hour grew at an average
annual rate of 3.3% in the nonfarm business sector of the
U.S., according to the Council of Economic Advisors. From
1965 to 1978, that rate of labor productivity growth was cut
in half, averaging 1.6% per year. In recent years the United
States has had the lowest rate of productivity growth of any

Table 2. International comparison relevant to labor and capital productivity performance, selected countries.

Country	Labor Productivity (% average annual growth in GNP per civilian employed)		Capital Productivity Ratio* (% average annual growth in GNP/year ÷ % average annual growth in fixed nonresidential investment)	
	1955–65	1965–71	1955–65 to 1953–63	1965–71 to 1963–69
United States	2.2	1.3	1.13	0.50
France	5.1	4.8	0.51	0.75
West Germany	4.5	4.3	0.56	0.80
Belgium–Luxembourg	2.7	3.7	0.59	0.85
Netherlands	3.1	4.3	0.62	0.63
Italy	5.6	5.5	0.63	4.42
United Kingdom	2.1	2.8	0.46	0.44
Canada	1.9	1.8	1.43	0.80
Japan	8.0	9.6	0.65	0.79
USSR	3.5	3.6	0.67	0.70

Source: Boretsky, M., "Trends in U.S. Technology: A Political Economist's View," *American Scientist* (January/February 1975), p. 72.

*Note: A two-year lag for the effects of new investment is assumed.

major noncommunist economy. Furthermore, the productivity growth collapse is accelerating. While the annual growth rate for 1965-73 averaged 2.1%, from 1973-78 it was 0.8%. In the first six months of 1979, output per labor-hour in the private business sector actually <u>fell</u> at an annual rate of 3.3%. During the second quarter of 1979, "productivity fell at an annual rate of 5.7%, the largest quarterly decline ever recorded in this series of statistics, which began in 1947."[24]

Boretsky presents an international comparison bearing on both capital and labor productivity growth among major industrial countries in two periods, 1955-65 and 1965-71. The results of his calculations are presented in Table 2. The performance of the U.S. is abysmal, both relative to its own historical performance, and relative to other nations. In the latter period, its labor productivity growth is the lowest of any nation compared, and only the United Kingdom shows a lower capital productivity growth ratio. Note particularly that the West German and Japanese performance is once again strong relative to the U.S. and other nations in the latter period, particularly in terms of labor productivity.

The fact of the productivity collapse is so overwhelming as to no longer be a matter of dispute. But its cause is still the source of much confusion and consternation. An article in the 19 October 1979 issue of <u>Science</u> by John Walsh bore witness to this situation. Its title and subtitle were: "Productivity Problems Trouble Economy--Everybody talks about the lag in the growth of productivity but nobody seems to know enough to do much about it." In the course of the article a number of candidates for cause of the productivity problem are cited: "Some economists assign major blame....to a shift to a 'service' economy"; "...the recent rise in energy costs"; "...the increase in government regulation"; "changing attitudes among workers...a new devotion to leisure and relaxation" (a euphemistic way of stating the lazy worker hypothesis); even sexist "...the labor force has become increasingly inexperienced because of an influx of women..." and racist "...the transformation of the U.S. economy is proceeding in the direction taken by the British rather than the Japanese. Anglo Saxon attitudes may produce a less pressured, less competitive way of life...." All these explanations have been given some credence.

The service sector argument is easily dismissed by the fact that productivity growth in U.S. manufacturing (i.e., excluding services) has been undergoing a similar pattern of deterioration. From 1947 to 1964, the average annual rate of

productivity increase in U.S. manufacturing was 4.1%; from
1965 to 1975 the average annual rate had dropped by more than
half to under 1.7% per year. As cited in the Walsh article
referred to above, Victor Fuchs of the National Bureau of
Economic Research has estimated that the growth of the
service sector contributed only about 0.1% to the decline in
productivity from the 1960's to the 1970's. Fuchs further
estimates a similar extremely small contribution to the influx of women.

Edward F. Denison, a senior fellow at the Brookings
Institution and a noted authority on productivity and economic growth has examined in detail and rejected a whole series
of commonly offered explanations for the productivity
problems as being responsible for too small a fraction of the
decline to have real significance. These include stiffer
environmental regulations, increased government paperwork,
lazy workers, declining Yankee ingenuity, etc.[25]

On the matter of research and development, Walsh points
out, "in the past, a belief that spending on R & D led to
innovation was widely, rather uncritically held in the U.S.
and used as blanket justification for government support of
R & D. The view came to be considered as oversimplified both
outside and inside government, and spending on R & D by
government declined."[26] Denison argues that cuts in research
and development spending are incapable of explaining the
productivity drop. On the other hand, Edwin Mansfield of the
University of Pennsylvania, another noted authority on productivity and in particular its relation to R & D has stated,
reflecting on 20 years of economic studies, "Research and
development seems to have had a very significant effect on
the rate of productivity growth in the industries and time
periods that have been studied."[27]

The fact is technological development does have an extremely important effect on productivity growth, if it is
civilian technological development oriented to such a
purpose. One cannot hope to see, and therefore cannot hope
to understand, the fundamental role of failing technological
progress in producing this present and ongoing productivity
deterioration in the U.S. until a clear and precise distinc-
tion is made between civilian and military related technological development. For it is most assuredly not the
failure of technology as a whole that has produced our
present productivity problems--the U.S. scientific and engineering community is not becoming less ingenious or less
productive. Rather the collapse is a direct, inevitable
though long-term result of the decades long diversion of a
large fraction of the nation's critical scientific and

engineering effort from productive civilian oriented technological development.

Productivity growth, inflation and unemployment. The
improvement in productivity plays a crucial role in the
countering of inflationary pressures, for it is sustained
productivity growth that offsets the effects of rising input
costs. It is not the separate cost of labor, fuels, materials, and capital that is relevant to the determination of
product price, but rather the combined cost of these productive resources per unit of product. Thus, the rise in
labor costs, for example, might be at least partially offset
by substituting cheaper capital for increasingly expensive
labor, or by organizing production to use labor more efficiently or both. As long as the net result is to produce
more output per unit of input, rises in input costs need not
be fully translated into rises in the cost per unit of
product. Correspondingly, the upward "cost-push" pressures
on price will be mitigated. But productivity is nothing more
than a measure of output per unit input. Hence rising productivity permits absorption of rising prices of labor, fuels,
etc. without full reflection of these resource cost increases
in unit cost and thus in price.

It is therefore clear that the deterioration of productivity growth will substantially compromise this cost offsetting capability. In the absence of strong productivity
improvement, rising costs of labor, fuels, etc. will be
translated into rising product prices. As this occurs over
a whole series of industries, a self-reinforcing rise in the
general level of prices or "inflation" occurs.

The mid 1960's was the breakpoint for the growth of
manufacturing productivity in the U.S. It should therefore
also have been the point of shift for cost behavior in U.S.
manufacturing industry from traditional "cost offsetting" or
"cost minimizing" behavior to the sort of "cost passalong"
or "cost indifferent" behavior just described--behavior in
which input cost increases are simply translated or "passed
along" into product price increases. A first empirical investigation of the possibility of this shift in modal cost
behavior was performed by Byung Hong, in doctoral research at
Columbia University.[28] Hong developed a simple multiple re-
gression model consisting of one price equation and one wage
equation which he fit to quarterly data for U.S. manufacturing
for two periods: 1948 (second quarter) to 1964 (fourth quarter) and 1965 (first quarter) to 1975 (second quarter).

In the price equation, the percentage change in wholesale prices was said to depend upon the percentage changes in

wages and raw materials costs moderated by changes in productivity, the level of capacity utilization (as a measure of demand pressure) and profit rates. Under conditions of cost offsetting behavior, the change in productivity would be expected to have a strong negative effect, as pressure was applied to improve productive efficiency in response to rising input costs, whereas under cost pass-along productivity growth would not be expected to have any significant impact on price increase. On the other hand, profit rate would have little effect on price under cost offsetting as compared to a clear positive effect under cost indifference, since profits are maintained or increased to a much greater extent by expansion of productivity in the former and by increase in price in the latter case. Furthermore, high capacity utilization would tend to lead to higher prices under cost offsetting ("demand pull") but lower prices under cost indifference because of lowered fixed cost per unit). Essentially all of the cost offset expectations are statistically supported in the earlier time period, and nearly all the expectations for cost indifference in the later time span.

In the wage equation, productivity change represents wage demand justification, past profits are wage demand targets, past consumer price inflation rates represent pressure for higher wages, and the unemployment rate is a kind of bargaining power variable. Under traditional cost offsetting behavior, the unemployment rate would be expected to have a significantly negative effect on wages, reflecting the Phillips curve type tradeoff, while no particular effect on wage increase would be expected under cost pass-along (since the source of inflation has nothing to do with demand pull pressures reflected in the unemployment rate). The consumer price variable would be stronger under cost pass-along than under cost offset as both rates of inflation and the price change expectations they generate are high and rising. All else held constant, a given increment in productivity growth might well have a larger effect on wage increase in a cost indifferent than in a cost offsetting environment because productivity growth would be so much weaker in such a period (a sort of decreasing marginal returns to productivity growth in terms of generating wage increases?). In any case, again nearly all of the expectations for cost offsetting behavior are statistically observed in the earlier period, and nearly all of the expectations for cost pass-along behavior are observed in the latter period, thus reinforcing the price equation results.

As the managements of U.S. industrial firms learned that cost indifference or passalong was a viable behavior, the incentives for the kind of internal vigilance necessary for cutting edge cost minimization were mitigated. And so, the decline of productivity growth was further exacerbated, reinforcing the shift to cost pass-along.

The implications of the productivity induced shift of modal cost behavior for stagflation are straightforward. As cost indifference became the order of the day, input cost increases were more and more rapidly and strongly translated into output price increases. And of course, via the usual wage price spiral augmented by external input cost increases (e.g. OPEC oil price actions) themselves perhaps partly engendered by output inflation, the process was made more severe. This has been a powerful inflationary engine. But the same mechanism has also generated unemployment.

As the prices of U.S. produced goods rose higher and higher, the nation's industry became less and less competitive vis-a-vis foreign competition. Overseas markets were lost and the U.S. export position weakened. Domestic markets were lost to foreign production and the U.S. import position worsened. The progressive loss of markets induced cutbacks in U.S.-based production with high unemployment rates the result. And this problem was exacerbated by the flight of U.S. owned production facilities to cheap labor havens abroad, as one logical response to the inability to offset higher costs in the U.S. because of the productivity failure. It is thus preeminently the declining competitiveness of U.S. industry resulting from decreasing productivity growth that has generated unemployment even in the face of high product demand.

Productivity growth thus is "the economic linchpin of the 1980's," as the Joint Economic Committee of the Congress described it in its mid-1979 analysis of prospects for the economy. Its warning that, as the New York Times put it, "The average American is likely to see his standard of living drastically reduced in the 1980's unless productivity growth is accelerated"[29] is precisely correct.

During the entire decade of the 1970's the dynamic process of deterioration which has been described here has produced the unprecedented simultaneous high inflation/high unemployment that has become a fact of our economic life. For an entire decade, the inflation rate has averaged near 7% at the same time the unemployment rate has averaged more than 6%.

The current military buildup being proposed by the Reagan Administration is, as Lester Thurow has pointed out,

three times as large as that which took place during the
Vietnam War. And it is taking place in a context of a much
weaker domestic economy than that of the 1960's, counterposed
against the economic strength of our chief economic adver-
saries (who are at the same time our military allies). In
Thurow's words,

> "When a nation such as the U.S. sharply increases its
> military forces, it generally does so at a time when
> its industrial competitors are also attempting to
> increase their own military establishments, and are
> experiencing comparable economic strains. But the
> Reagan buildup is to take place in a time when our
> allies are not raising their military expenditures
> at anything like our pace....This difference poses
> the problem of how the U.S. can maintain the indus-
> trial strength to compete with other countries in
> civilian production and sales."[30]

The economic prognosis for the coming decade is not good.
If the arms race continues unabated, and we somehow manage to
survive, these rates of inflation and unemployment--rates
that were viewed as horrific at the beginning of the 1970's--
may well look like economic good times compared to what will
be commonplace by the end of the 1980's.

As damaging as the persistence of high levels of military spending has been to the domestic economy, and as
dependent economic revitalization might be on a reversal of
this situation, it is nevertheless true that the process of
transition to a more fully civilian-oriented economy must be
handled carefully. Producing a smooth economic conversion
requires a clear understanding of the nature of the multi-
faceted transition problem. The solution to that problem
lies at the core of the political economic strategy that is
a key prerequisite to the linked process of reversing the
present economic decay, particularly in the U.S. and USSR,
and achieving real, meaningful arms reduction. It is to that
problem that attention is now turned.

References

1.   Dumas, Lloyd J., "National Insecurity in the Nuclear
     Age," *Bulletin of the Atomic Scientists* (May, 1976) and
     "Human Fallibility and Weapons," *Bulletin of the Atomic
     Scientists* (November, 1980).

2.   Dumas, Lloyd J., "Armament, Disarmament and National
     Security: A Theoretical Duopoly Model of the Arms Race,"
     Journal of Economic Studies (May, 1979).

3. York, Herbert F., <u>Race to Oblivion: A Participant's View of the Arms Race</u>, Simon & Shuster, 1970 (see especially Chapter 12).

4. Bureau of Economic Analysis, U.S. Department of Commerce, <u>Business Statistics</u> (1973) p. 69.

5. Ibid, p. 40.

6. For example, the Air Force's C5A transport plane, which experienced a $2 billion cost overrun (i.e. excess of actual cost over original cost estimates) was produced under a firm "fixed price" contract. Payment was simply adjusted upward to cover the overrun. Thus, the fixed price was fixed in name only. A number of fascinating "insiders" accounts of the operation of military procurement are available that document in detail these practices. Two such accounts are: <u>The High Priests of Waste</u> (New York: W. W. Norton, 1972) by A. Ernest Fitzgerald, former Air Force Deputy for Management Systems in the Pentagon (this includes much detail on the C5A); and <u>Arming America: How the U.S. Buys Weapons</u> (Boston: Harvard University Press, 1974) by J. Ronald Fox, former Assistant Secretary of the Army (for procurement).

7. Dumas, Lloyd J. "Payment Functions and the Productive Efficiency of Military Industrial Firms," <u>Journal of Economic Issues</u> (June, 1976)

8. National Science Board, National Science Foundation, <u>Science Indicators</u>: 1978 (Washington: U.S. Government Printing Office, 1979), p. 182.

9. National Science Foundation, Surveys of Science Resources Series, <u>Characteristics of the National Sample of Scientists and Engineers</u>: 1974, <u>Part 2: Employment</u>, Table B-16 (pp. 128-142).

10. Ibid., Table B-15 (pp. 113-127).

11. Ibid., Table B-10 (pp. 85-89).

12. National Science Foundation, "Full-Time Equivalent Number of R & D Scientists and Engineers, by Industry and Source of Funds for R & D Projects: January, 1975 and January, 1976" (Table 93).

13. National Academy of Engineering Committee on Technology Transfer and Utilization "Technology Transfer and

26   Lloyd J. Dumas

Utilization, Recommendations for Reducing the Emphasis
and Correcting the Imbalance" (Washington, D.C.:
National Academy, 1974), p. i.

14. National Science Board, National Science Foundation,
Science Indicators: 1974 (Washington: U.S. Government
Printing Office, 1976) p. 17.

15. Ibid., p. 19.

16. Op. cit., NSF Science Indicators: 1978, p. 2.

17. Ibid, p. 18.

18. Ibid, pp. 20-21.

19. Ibid, pp. 19-20.

20. Ibid, pp. 146-147.

21. Boretsky, Michael, "Trends in U.S. Technology: A
Political Economist's View," American Scientist
(January/February, 1975) p. 76.

22. Op. cit, NSF, Science Indicators: 1978, pp. 78-79.

23. Op. cit, Boretsky, p. 70.

24. Farnsworth, Clyde H., "Lag in Productivity Called Major
Peril to Living Standard," New York Times (August 13,
1979).

25. Denison, Edward F., Accounting for Slower Economic
Growth: The U.S. in the 1970's (Washington, D.C.: The
Brookings Institution, 1979).

26. Walsh, John, "Productivity Problems Trouble Economy,"
Science (19 October, 1979) p. 311.

27. Ibid.

28. Hong, Byung, Inflation Under Cost Pass-Along Management
(New York: Praeger, 1979).

29. Op. cit., Farnsworth.

30. Thurow, Lester, "How to Wreck the Economy," New York
Review of Books (May 14, 1981)

2. The Conversion of Military Economy: The United States

Introduction

The persistence of high levels of military spending over the last three and a half decades of what has officially been called "peacetime" has been a primary source of the on-going stagflation from which the U.S. has suffered since 1969. It is therefore inconceivable that more than fleeting, cosmetic improvements in the economic situation in the U.S. can be achieved while the military budget is being expanded. In fact, substantial reductions in military spending, along with the transference of resources now in the military sector of the economy to productive, civilian-oriented activity, are prerequisite to returning the U.S. economy to health and vigor. Such transference has been called "economic conversion," and the problem of carrying it out smoothly and efficiently so as to replace the previous military activity not merely with some civilian alternative activity but with economically viable alternative activity is the main focus of this present chapter. This must, of course, begin with a thorough understanding of the parameters of the process.

The Nature of the Conversion Problem

The difficulty of transferring resources smoothly between any given pair of activities depends on two factors: (1) the volume of resources to be so transferred; and (2) the degree of similarity between the activities. Transition difficulty depends positively on the former, and negatively on the latter. Since the volume of resources being transferred is a function of the extensivity of the conversion problem upon which we are focusing (i.e. are we dealing with one small facility or taking a more macro nationwide view), while the second factor is relevant at all levels, it is this latter factor on which attention will be concentrated here.

Technological resource conversion. A major part of the
problem of converting technologists from military to civilian
oriented work is rooted in the differential requirements for
successful military and civilian technological development.
Present day high technology military products are extremely
complex, and are designed with an effort to squeeze every
possible ounce of performance out of the product. Whether
or not this extra performance capability actually has military significance, the presumption that it does clearly
underlies the practice of weapons research and development.
This has led to the assignment of large teams of technologists
to the design of weapons systems, each, in effect, developing and designing a part of a part. Accordingly, the need
to become expert in a very narrow range of knowledge has led
to extreme specialization of engineers and scientists
engaged in military-related work. In addition, the extreme
priority attached to military funding, combined with the
common practice of procuring weapons on an effectively cost-
plus basis and the pressure for even small increments in
weapons capability, has led to strong emphasis on the cost
implications of design. In fact more expensive designs will
certainly result in increases in sales revenue and typically
in profit as well to the firms which generate them.

Successful design for the civilian market place, on the
other hand, requires very heavy emphasis on the implications
of the specific design for the cost of producing the ultimate
product. This implies that designers, rather than being
extremely specialized, should have a fairly clear concept of
the overall design of the product and the interactions of its
subcomponents. This, together with a basic understanding of
the effects on cost of modifying the design in one way or
another, will enable them to trade off changes in one part
of the design against changes in the other to achieve desired
product performance at the lowest possible cost. Keeping
production cost down enables the price to be kept at a level
which will make the product attractive to potential customers
and hence bring expanded sales and profit to the firm.

Because of these differences, engineers and scientists
performing defense work must be retrained and re-oriented
before they can be successful in civilian research and
development. Complete retraining is clearly not required,
since much of the mathematical, scientific, and engineering
knowledge they already have is also required for civilian
work. But despecialization and increased cost sensitivity
are required to establish firm connection with civilian
design realities.

The length of the retraining process depends on the
specific individual involved, the nature of his/her previous

education and experience and the particular pair of activities between which the transfer is taking place. Clearly, a civil engineer moving between design work on jet fighters and design work on corporate jets will require less extensive retraining than one transferring from jet fighter design to bridge building. Yet it is possible to give a reasonably generalized range estimate for retraining time. It is unlikely to require less than six months or more than two years. In all likelihood, retraining and reorientation will ordinarily take a year to a year and a half.

The conversion process must also be extended to the educational institutions responsible for the training of engineers and scientists. These institutions have altered their curricula to emphasize specialization, especially in areas and sub-areas of interest to the military, and strongly de-emphasize training in cost-related matters. Instruction in mundane civilian-oriented areas like, for example, power engineering, was curtailed or eliminated, particularly at the "best" schools. All this may have been an appropriate institutional response to the changing shape of the high prestige opportunities available to their graduates. And yet, these changes meant that even those engineers and scientists who did go directly into civilian areas were to some extent less than optimally trained for the development of civilian-oriented technological progress. Existing engineering and scientific institutions, once reoriented themselves, should be fully competent to carry out transitional retraining of the sort needed to produce a smooth and efficient conversion process.

The inability of military-oriented engineers and scientists to move into civilian-oriented research and development without conversion retraining is indicated by the commonly observed tendency of technologists, laid off because of the termination of a defense contract to move to another geographic area to follow the contracts, accept nonengineering or nonscientific work, or simply remain unemployed until the contracts return. This tendency has been read by some as an indication that civilian technology is not starved by the diversion of technological personnel to military areas as I have argued, since they are not grabbed up by civilian research programs when they do become unemployed. But the failure of these technologists to be readily absorbed into civilian industry is due to the inappropriateness of their training and experience, not an overall lack of demand and certainly not a lack of national or commercial need. This point is periodically illustrated by such events as the development of a critical shortage of engineers qualified to design new non-nuclear power plants in the early 1970's side by side with the existence of a substantial pool of unemployed military-oriented engineers.[1]

Management conversion. The management of military industrial firms operate in a very different atmosphere from that which prevails in civilian-oriented enterprise. Defense firms have, in practice, only one customer -- the United States Government. They cannot sell their products to civilian customers in any case, and can sell to foreign governments only with the direct and specific approval of the U.S. Department of Defense. Even so, weapons sold to foreign governments were originally designed, developed, and produced for sale to the U.S. Government.

The one-customer orientation produces a very different sales and marketing situation from that faced by civilian firms. Rather than knowing how to run an effective electronic and print media advertising campaign, how to survey markets for public acceptance of a new product line, how to price a product for penetration into new markets or expansion of existing ones, etc., it becomes critical to know the minute detail of the Armed Services Procurement Regulations, to develop good working relationships with key government procurement personnel, and to be able to lobby effectively with members of the Congress.

Furthermore, the military industrial firm sells its product before it is produced, a very different situation from that faced by typical civilian manufacturers. This, combined with the availability of "progress payments," i.e. installment payments made by the government as different stages of the production process are completed, greatly alters the nature of the financing function, substantially lowering the need for equity funds. (This, of course, also tends to make the rate of return on equity, the conventional measure of profit rate, extremely high in military firms.)

Another critical difference is that the single customer does not itself have to sell its product in a market place. It does not therefore have to worry either about the effects on the ultimate price of its "product," of paying too much for the goods it buys, or the danger of its being forced into loss or bankruptcy by a drop in its sales if the equipment it purchases does not perform well.[2]

This strongly interacts with a third critical factor, the extremely high priority accorded to defense procurement, currently supported by national public consensus. This not only assures that the Defense Department will continue to be a very rich customer, but also that its purchase decisions will be readily validated by both the Congress and the President. Thus, the wealthy customer that military industry services faces no economic market test, and only the very loosest political constraints.

The net effect of these last two factors has been to guarantee at least higher revenues and typically higher profits to those military firms which are most effective in running up the cost of the products which they are contracted to produce, often regardless of whether or not these products perform as they were supposed to. A management operating in such milieu will become very effective at finding ways of producing at high cost. But this sort of management training and experience is completely inappropriate to successful operation in civilian markets, where holding costs down is the crucial skill.

One of the most striking examples of the contrast between the way in which products get produced for military as opposed to civilian markets lies in the comparison of the Boeing 747 and the Lockheed C5A cargo plane. Both of these are jumbo jets of roughly comparable size, but the former was designed and produced for sale to commercial civilian airlines and the latter for sale to the U.S. Air Force. The 747 is a smooth flying, highly reliable aircraft flown daily by most of the world's major airlines, and is as energy efficient when fully loaded as a Volkswagen "beetle" carrying only its driver. The C5A has been plagued by severe operating difficulties, including cracking of the wing pylons, crash-producing failures of the rear cargo door, and considerable landing gear problems. The Air Force has acknowledged that a cargo version of the 747 could carry a larger payload than the C5A.[3] In 1971, the 747 was selling at about $23 million per plane as against the $60 million per plane cost of the C5A.[4] Furthermore, the wing defects on the C5A, which reduced its estimated service life by more than 70%, were projected to cost some $1.3 billion to repair, nearly doubling the original cost estimates for the program.[5]

That managements of military firms are in a sense rewarded for high cost production, even in the face of low product quality and performance, is illustrated by the following listing of article headlines, excerpted from the New York Times:

(1) "Nine Spy Planes Lost in Crashes, Pentagon Says" (March 23, 1979)...these planes were developed by Lockheed.

(2) "X Factor Continues to Raise Luftwaffe's Starfighter Toll" (July 4, 1972)...report of the 154th crash of this plane designed by Lockheed.

(3) "Lockheed's Step Is Costliest Ever: $800 Million Write-Off on Tristar..." (November 23, 1974)...

report of financial loss by Lockheed in its
development of the L1011 commercial jet.

(4) "C5A Jet Repairs to Cost $1.5 Billion"
(December 5, 1975).

(5) "Lockheed Rises to Top as Defense Contractor"
(December 11, 1975).

And, of course, this is the same firm whose management
was granted a $250 million loan guarantee by the Federal
Government.

Clearly, one cannot expect managers accustomed to operating in a situation in which there is no risk, high costs
are not merely tolerated but become the path to success, and
only one rich customer need be serviced, to operate successfully in risky, cost sensitive, multi-customer civilian
markets without substantial retraining and re-orientation.
When unconverted military industrial managements have turned
their attention to production of civilian products for state
and local governments, the results have borne a striking
resemblance to their military operations in both cost and
performance. Consider, for example, the Bay Area Rapid
Transit (BART) system in San Francisco whose prime contractor was the Rohr Company, a firm which made its reputation
in aerospace and related operations. Although the system
was supposed to be in operation by 1968, prototypes were
still crashing in 1971.[6] A few weeks after it opened in
1972, the computer-controlled network experienced a number
of breakdowns, including one instance in which a train
"failed to slow down at the end of the line, barreled
through a sand barrier, and did a nosedive into a parking
lot."[6] As of late 1975, up to half the cars were out of
service at any given time, "causing delays and standing room
only for San Francisco commuters, who have dubbed it Bay
Area Reckless Transit."[7] By 1971, estimates for the cost of
the system had grown from $792 million to $1.4 billion.[8]

There is little question, that whether military oriented
managements are turned to the supervision of the production
of goods and services sold in the civilian market place or
for civilian use by government, they must be retrained and
re-oriented as a prerequisite for successful conversion.

For managers, as for engineers and scientists, the
length of the retraining process for any given individual
depends upon that particular person's education and experience, though it is likely to be somewhat less sensitive in
the managerial than in the technological case. Similarly,
the nature of the activities between which transference is

being made influences both the length and nature of the
retraining. In general it is likely that the retraining and
re-orientation period will take on the order of six to
eighteen months. Existing business and related schools at
universities around the country should be capable of carrying out this transitional educational process, most likely
with less internal readjustment than would be required at
institutions engaged in retraining engineers and scientists.
Management training centers of various large civilian-oriented
corporations should also be available to aid in the process.

Conversion of production and low-level administrative
workers. With the possible exception of a few highly
skilled workers, the primary problem in channeling production and administrative workers into civilian oriented work
lies not in the need for re-education but rather in the
numbers of people involved. Roughly six million people in
the United States are directly employed in military-related
work by the Pentagon, and by military-oriented industry.
Clearly, the bulk of these employees are production workers
and low level administrative employees, including clerical
workers.

Re-orientation to the standards of work of civilian
enterprises will undoubtedly be required, since the lack of
pressure toward efficiency generated by cost plus pricing
permeates the system, and it is possible that additional
vocational training will be required for some of these
employees. This latter training is not so much to undo the
effects of having been employed in military-related work as
such (as in the case of engineers, scientists and managers),
but rather to bring their skills into more perfect congru-
ence with the best civilian opportunities available. The
transition problem is simpler here because of the lesser
nature of the re-education required, but more difficult
because many more people are potentially involved.

The civilian re-employment of the workers displaced by
cutbacks in military expenditures creates a potential problem for the unions involved, since workers may be transferred
into industries or lines of work in the ordinary jurisdiction
of unions other than those to which they currently belong.
The seriousness of this problem depends on the particular
form of organization of the unions involved, craft unions
being clearly less likely to be affected than industrial
unions. What with teamsters organizing teachers and the
steelworkers organizing workers at nuclear weapons facilities
these days the problem has been somewhat mitigated. Nevertheless, this issue must be taken seriously, among other
reasons if one is to avoid opposition to economic conversion
by leaders of unions with an inordinately short-term and

parochial view. As we have seen, continued high military
expenditure is economically destructive, and in the longer
term its inflation and unemployment-generating effects hurt
defense workers as well as the large numbers of nondefense
workers who constitute the vast majority of the U.S. labor
force.

Capital equipment and facilities. Some of the industrial equipment and facilities currently employed in the
service of the military are sufficiently general purpose in
nature to be directly usable in civilian-oriented work. But
some, such as certain types of extremely high capability
machine tools, specialized shipbuilding facilities and highly
specialized equipment for working with extraordinarily toxic
materials (such as plutonium) are not so directly trans-
ferable. As to machinery whose civilian applicability
suffers mainly from the excessive cost derived from its
excessively high performance capability, the equipment should
be usable for civilian operations if some sort of special
one-time write-offs or tax breaks are allowed to overcome the
cost penalty.

Those industrial facilities which do not so much possess
excess capabilities as the wrong capabilities will have to be
reconstructed, but that cannot be effectively done until
specific plans have been developed for the particular alternative purpose to which those facilities are to be turned.
Similarly, military bases are unlikely to be appropriate,
without some degree of alteration, for efficient performance
of a civilian oriented activity.

Nuclear weapons facilities represent an interesting
special case. In planning for conversion of nuclear weapons
facilities there tend to be two common problems specifically
related to the physical facility. The first is the existence
of plant and equipment highly specialized to the storage,
handling and processing of nuclear materials. At the manufacturing end (places like the Rocky Flats Plant near
Denver), there may be glove boxes, dust and fume control
devices, remote manipulators, etc. At the storage and ship-
ping end (places like the Seal Beach Naval Weapons Station
near Los Angeles), there are earth-covered storage bunkers,
special handling containers, etc. And at the waste storage
facilities (like those in Hanford, Washington), large--and
now thoroughly contaminated--tanks and associated facilities
are found. This leads directly to the second problem, the
problem of radioactive contamination.

It would be extremely surprising if there were a single
nuclear weapons facility that was untouched by continuing

radiation problems. It is certain that manufacturing
facilities and waste facilities dealing with nuclear materials house at least some equipment that is heavily contam-
inated. In addition, leakages of radioactive materials into
the soil at all such locations are a virtual certainty,
rendering portions of the site and perhaps associated water
supplies hazardous. The extent to which it is possible to
effectively de-contaminate this equipment and these areas
can only be determined by a thorough analysis of each
facility. If there are storage areas from which nuclear
materials cannot be removed for health, safety or whatever
reasons, extreme care must be taken to avoid establishing
new activity on the site that could threaten their integrity.
And if such materials have already been lost into the immediate environment, care must be taken to avoid further
dispersal in the process of modifying the facility or in the
nature of the new activity to be established there.

The meaning of both these problems is that some parts
of nuclear weapons facilities may have to be reckoned as a
dead loss in planning conversion. But this is not equivalent to saying that activities carried on at such facilities
are non-convertible. Even if the whole physical facility
were unusable for productive civilian alternatives (a rare
event), the labor force is an extremely valuable resource.

Preparing capital equipment and facilities for conversion is primarily a matter of assessing in detail what
changes in layout, direct equipment and facilities, and
supporting equipment and facilities are implied by the
chosen civilian alternative. Given such an assessment, it
should not be difficult to estimate both financing requirements and the time needed from start to finish for the
actual physical conversion. This will in turn enable development of a financial plan, as well as effective coordination
of this phase of the resource conversion process with the
others.

Intra-regional concentration and the conversion problem.
Property taxes, which were the subject of the famed taxpayer
revolt of 1978 that began with the passage of Proposition 13
in California, constitute only about one-fifth of the average
individual's tax burden. These taxes flow to state and local
governments, primarily to finance local services such as
education, road repair, health care, police, fire and sanitation services, as well as public welfare. Federal income
taxes, on the other hand, are responsible for nearly half
the individual's direct tax burden. Almost two-thirds of
what the U.S. Office of Management and Budget defines as
"relatively controllable" federal outlays (those essentially

decided upon year-by-year) went for military purposes. In
1977, the average U.S. citizen paid $2.50 in federal income
tax for every dollar paid in state and local property tax.
Thus, the part of the individual's tax burden taken as "military tax" can be roughly estimated as somewhere between $1.10
and $1.60 per dollar of property tax.

While the incidence of military tax corresponds
essentially to the pattern of per capita income, the military
expenditures which the tax supports are distributed in a very
different pattern. Military spending tends to be concentrated in relatively distinct geographic pockets, which are to be
found in all major geographic sectors of the U.S. Examples
include the San Francisco Bay area, Seattle, the Dallas-Fort
Worth metroplex, and the Boston-Cambridge area. This combination of high concentration and geographic dispersion has
important political and economic implications.

Politically, one would be hard-pressed to devise a
geographic pattern which would provide better leverage. The
Congressional representatives elected by constituencies which
include one or more of these pockets, feel themselves compelled to support military programs that they perceive are
in the interest of the people by whom they were elected,
providing them with continued employment. They come to
believe that their continued election depends upon the
effectiveness with which they can aid in at least maintaining, if not expanding the flow of military funds to their
district. Accordingly, they may become salespeople for the
military industry in their area.

Geographic concentration guarantees that the impact of
alterations in the pattern, and particularly the magnitude,
of military expenditure will not go unnoticed. The geographic dispersion of these pockets maximizes the likelihood
that, through the normal process of congressional quid pro
quo vote trading, support for maintenance or expansion of
military expenditures will continue. This is particularly
true to the extent that military spending pockets are
focused in the districts of key Congresspeople.

In a recent study, James Anderson of Michigan State
University analyzed the distribution of direct military tax
dollar burden counterposed against the distribution of
military spending by state, major metropolitan area and by
congressional district.[9]

When both the military expenditure inflows and the
military tax outflows are taken into consideration the usual
picture of military spending as a broad-gauge boon to the

nation's economy takes on a different cast, for the pattern
is one of vastly unequal distribution of burdens and
benefits. A total of 305 of the nation's 435 congressional
districts are, according to Anderson's calculations, net
losers. Of all the east coast states, only Maryland and
Connecticut have more congressional districts with net inflow
than outflow. Not a single state in the entire mid-country
has more net inflow than outflow districts; the same is true
of the South, where even Texas, second in the nation in total
prime military contracts, has 14 out of 24 districts which
are net losers. The two regions of the U.S. experiencing the
greatest economic stagnation difficulties, the Northeast and
the Midwest, are severely drained: 79 of the 104 congressional districts in the Northwest are net losers, as are 95
of the 100 districts in the upper Midwest.[10]

Within states, the disparities can be extreme. In
Mississippi, for example, the state as a whole has a net
excess of military spending over military tax of $1.3
billion. Yet, in Anderson's words, "Four out of its five
congressional districts, comprising the northern four-fifths
of the state's population and land area suffer a net drain.
. . About $1.6 billion of Pentagon spending is concentrated
entirely within the southeastern corner of the state. . ."[11]
Texas, too is a case in point. The Dallas-Fort Worth and
San Antonio metropolitan areas experienced net inflows in
fiscal 1977 of $862 million and $932 million, respectively,
at the same time that the military tax burden was producing
a net drain of $964 million in Houston.

It is not the intention here to analyze in any great
detail the status and power in the Congress of the representatives of the net inflow areas, particularly in the
House of Representatives where sheer numbers and complexity
greatly magnify the task. However, a quick look at the 96th
Congress, i.e., that which held office just _prior_ to the
sharp conservative pro-military shift that accompanied the
Reagan election of 1980, indicates some interesting, though
highly tentative results.[12] The largest net gain congressional district in the nation (nearly $1.6 billion) was, and
is, that of Congressman Wright of Texas, the House Majority
Leader. Nearly a dozen Representatives from the top 50 net
inflow districts sat on the House Armed Services Committee;
9 sat on the Budget, Appropriations, or Ways and Means
Committees, a dozen more on the Rules or Government Operations Committees. But, on the whole, the picture in the
House was sufficiently ambiguous to require a much closer
look before drawing firm conclusions.

In the Senate, the picture was a bit simpler and more

clear. The ten states which had the largest net inflows
according to the Anderson study were (in descending order):
California, Virginia, Texas, Missouri, Connecticut,
Mississippi, Washington, Hawaii, New Mexico and Maryland.
Among the senators from these states were: the Senate
Majority Whip; the Chair, Ranking Minority Member and three
other members of the Armed Services Committee; the Chair of
the Appropriations Committee and the Chair of its Defense
Appropriations Subcommittee; and the Chair and five other
members of the Governmental Affairs Committee. It is also
interesting to note that 12 of the 17 members of the Armed
Services Committee represented net inflow states, and only
two represented a state without a single net inflow district
(Iowa) -- there are 12 such states.

What emerges here is a reasonably clear indication that
in terms of direct dollar tax outflows and offsetting direct
dollar return flows of military expenditures, the vast
majority of the nation suffers a net loss even when viewed
in simplistic, money flow terms. The military tax, offset
against expenditures, produces a net dollar drain in more
than 70% of the nation's congressional districts. Furthermore, a cursory glance at the Congress, even prior to its
new conservative tilt, gives some indication (particularly
in the Senate) that the pattern of expenditure relative to
taxation has either resulted in or been caused by a substantial congressional power base of representatives of areas
with direct and substantial political economic stake in
military expenditure decisions, and a clear upward bias for
reasons not necessarily related to either national security
realities or the general economic wellbeing of the nation.

The primary economic implication of the geographic
pattern of military-related facilities is that macroeconomic
policies such as income tax reductions and money supply
increases cannot cope with the problem of stimulating the
economy so as to effectively produce a smooth absorption of
the resources freed from military use into civilian activities. Such policies average their effects broadly over the
nation. But what is required here are policies which will
reach specifically into these pockets of military concentration and redevelop them. Only in this way can the temporary
economic dislocation which accompanies any major structural
change be held to a minimum, and the economic reconstruction
of the United States thus accomplished without real hardship.

Policies for Successful Conversion

An economically and socially successful conversion
process requires considerable planning and preparation.

First, a careful analysis must be performed to identify
appropriate civilian alternatives into which the resources
released from military-related activities may be effectively
channeled. Second, a program for efficiently preparing the
resources for their new civilian-oriented functions must be
carefully developed. Finally, in the case of the human
resources involved, various social services must be provided
during the period of transition including income maintenance,
employment services, and relocation and educational assistance where required. Consider each of these problems in
turn.

Civilian alternatives for military-related resources.
In a broad policy sense, it is not at all difficult to
identify economically and socially productive alternatives
for the employment of resources now devoted to unproductive
military use. One need only consider those vital social
services and important areas of the economic infrastructure
that are either presently in an advanced state of decline or
clearly undergoing serious progressive retrenchment. Urban
mass transit, housing, intercity rail transportation, police
and fire services, mental and physical health care, standard
education and vocational training, special education, care
for the elderly, day care, etc., all would benefit enormously from a transfusion of resources from military programs,
and that would clearly produce a major increase in the
nation's economic and social welfare.

Besides such directly socially conscious alternatives,
general redirection of resources into the production of
"standard of living" goods and services, from machine tools
to bubble gum, would revitalize the civilian economy. This
revitalization would play a major role in creating the
conditions under which the goal of full employment without
significant inflation becomes economically achievable. And
major gains in social welfare would clearly follow this kind
of economic redevelopment.

But while broad prescriptions are important from the
viewpoint of policy and perspective, an effective conversion
process requires the detailed specification of particular
alternatives for each facility, and each area undergoing
this transformation.

The first step is to analyze the nature and quantity of
all the productive resources involved in the transformation:
the types and numbers of machines and their capabilities,
the sorts of buildings (including their layout), the skill
and experience mix of the labor force, and the characteristics of the site, including its size, terrain and location.

The second step is to lay out a list of alternatives whose requirements for productive resources most closely correspond with what is currently available, as indicated by the resource analysis of the first step. Seeking alternatives which best match the capabilities of the present mix of resources minimizes dislocation and disruption by reducing the need for labor force hiring, firing, and retraining, and new equipment purchases. This tends to minimize the social cost of transition, as well as its direct financial cost. Furthermore, playing to the strengths of existing capabilities also increases the probability of success in the new activities. To some extent, the initial resource analysis will in itself suggest at least broad classes of feasible alternatives. For example, a manufacturing firm which owns considerable metalworking equipment and employs a fair amount of machinists would be more likely to convert successfully to the manufacture of metal office furniture or railroad cars than to the production of detergents or cosmetics.

This list of alternatives should not be conceived in purely industrial terms. Public and private nonmanufacturing projects, in areas such as pollution control, education, transportation, etc. are also major alternative productive uses of resources. For example, it may well be that the prime civilian-oriented use for a particular naval facility may be as a major sewage treatment complex, medical center, or new university campus, rather than as an industrial park. It would be a serious mistake to think too narrowly at this critical stage of developing alternatives.

Finally, the "success potential" of each of the alternatives should be evaluated. In the case of conversion of industrial facilities to civilian production this primarily involves a study of what is called the "marketability" of the product, which involves an analysis of the demand for the product at the ranges of price that would permit a sufficient margin of profit (after covering costs) to make this product line attractive to the producer. In the case of public or non-profit projects, the evaluation should involve an analysis of the social need for such a project in that region, as well as its estimated cost. In either case, the accuracy and realism of estimates of both one-time conversion costs and subsequent continuing post-conversion production costs play a critical role in determining the feasibility and attractiveness of any proposed alternative.

To the extent that there is less than a perfect match between the labor requirements of even the best civilian alternatives for a given military enterprise and its pre-conversion labor force, there will be a need to channel some

of the labor force into productive civilian activities
wholly outside of that particular enterprise. For example,
it is extremely unlikely that all or even most of the
engineers and scientists currently employed by military
industries would be required for any reasonable civilian
alternative activities to which these industries would turn.
This is no particular problem, in the sense that there are
many civilian activities outside these particular converted
industries in which the services of such personnel would be
of great value. We need to think in terms of sufficient
alternatives to productively re-employ all of the resources
(particularly labor) released from military activity, and
not simply sufficient alternatives to convert present military bases and military-industrial firms into civilian
facilities.

A Combine of unions representing workers at Lucas
Aerospace, one of the largest aerospace firms in Europe
(headquartered in the United Kingdom) has through the joint
efforts of its organized engineers and shop floor production
workers, produced a collection of alternative products
tailored to the Lucas facilities and workforce. Known as
the "Corporate Plan," this proposed set of alternatives
consists not only of civilian products in general, but of
what the Combine has called "socially useful" products in
particular. A detailed discussion of this extraordinary
initiative can be found in Chapter Six.

Transition support services. Workers undergoing occupational transition, whether or not it is part of a process of
conversion from military to civilian economy, must find ways
of connecting with new job opportunities, getting whatever
retraining is necessary, financing a move when relocation is
required, and keeping body and soul together during the
period between jobs. The burden of meeting all these needs
can be greatly eased by the availability of appropriate
social services.

Not all of the workers involved in the conversion
process will be changing employers, and those who will not
do not have to worry about locating new job opportunities or
maintaining their income. They may or may not require
retraining, and probably will not require relocation, but
even when retraining or re-location is necessary it should
be possible to finance them at least partially through
employers, though perhaps with some public supplementation.

Those individuals who must change employers will
generally have much greater need for social services.
Besides direct income maintenance assistance, they will

likely require temporary public replacement of some employment fringe benefits -- in particular group medical and
dental insurance plans. An effective public program of
employment services will be critical in making them aware of
the nature and location of the new employment opportunities
which best match their skills. Along with counseling
services, this will be of vital importance in enabling them
to plan whatever specific retraining they may need. In
addition, the employment service will facilitate the process
of direct placement of dislocated employees into new jobs.
To make the transition even smoother, the government could
provide special tax or other incentives for employers to sign
conditional employment contracts with potential employees
during this period that in effect guaranteed the prospective
employees a job with that organization upon successful completion of a mutually agreed upon program of retraining. In
this way, individuals requiring retraining that could be
expected to stretch over a period of time from six months to
a year would have some assurance that undertaking training
into a particular area of civilian expertise would provide
them with attractive re-employment. Aside from any direct
government benefits, private enterprises (whether businesses
or private nonprofit institutions) would gain from the increased certainty in planning such agreements would imply.

Operating the entire conversion process along the lines
suggested will tend to minimize the amount of geographic
relocation required. This is important because moves over
extended distances tend to be very disruptive of family and
friendship ties. While people develop social roots after
living in an area for a prolonged period, their ability to
re-establish roots in a new area should not be underestimated. This is particularly true of young people, who often
actively seek a new area in which to live and grow. In fact,
the general population of the United States is normally very
geographically mobile. For example, in 1970 nearly 50% of
the U.S. population lived in a different house than that in
which they lived in 1965, and nearly 25% of this group had
moved to a different state.[10]

At any rate, the high degree of geographic concentration
of military-related facilities virtually guarantees that some
relocation will be required for some individuals. This is
particularly true for engineers and scientists since they are
concentrated within pockets of defense industry much more
highly than they would be likely to be in any civilian-
oriented industry. But, the engineers and scientists who
work in military industry have already developed a pattern of
extraordinarily high geographic mobility as a result of their
occupational need to follow the shifting defense contracts.

So the prospect of one more move, coupled with the enhanced
likelihood of future geographic stability, should not be,
for them, an overly difficult thing with which to cope.

Expenses incurred in relocation for the purpose of re-
employment in a new area are already tax deductible as a
matter of course. Supplemental government relocation allowances for one time, conversion-connected single moves, along
with aid in locating new housing, should go far in further
easing the difficulties of relocating for those who must do
so.

It is extremely important to the successful revitalization of the U.S. economy and society that the conversion
process have a defined end. In order to avoid establishing
new kinds of unhealthy dependencies, any effective conversion
process must be designed to put itself out of business. The
permanent existence of a very small version of the machinery
for easing economic transitions may be of real value in a
dynamic economy, but great care must be taken to avoid giving
birth to large, new self-perpetuating conversion bureau-
cracies.

During each of the past several years, a bill containing
one model for institutionalizing effective conversion planning has been introduced into both houses of Congress. The
bill, called the Defense Economic Adjustment Act, embodies
a local authority, low bureaucracy, people-oriented conversion planning concept. The full text of the original
version of this bill is reprinted in Appendix A to this
chapter. Appendix B, "Questions and Answers about Economic
Conversion and the Defense Economic Adjustment Act" specifically addresses a number of the most common points raised in
the lengthy series of informal discussions that accompanied
the introduction of the bill.

The Defense Economic Adjustment Act is looked upon as
one model for achieving effective ongoing conversion planning
on a contingency basis. It is put forth in that spirit here,
with full acknowledgment that in this area too there are
undoubtedly a number of other workable alternative formula-
tions.

The bill would require the establishment of a tripartite
Alternative Use Committee at every military base and military
industrial facility in the U.S., consisting of one-third
representatives of the workforce at that facility, one-third
representatives of the facility's management and one-third
representatives of the local community without direct connection to that facility. These local committees would be

funded independently and would have complete control over
the process of drawing up conversion plans for their
facility. The diverse interests of each of the three groups
would combine to insure a serious planning effort.

The local Alternative Use Committees would be provided
with access to all information at the facility which they
would need to develop the plan. They would also be supplied
with a Conversion Guidelines Handbook produced by a central,
national Defense Economic Adjustment Council.

This national council (consisting of one third each
Cabinet members, representatives of nondefense business, and
labor unions), with a maximum staff of 15 persons, would
serve mainly to encourage the preparation of civilian public
projects at the Federal, State and local levels--projects
which could create markets for converted defense contractors.
It would also serve as an information coordinator. Though
the council may serve an advisory function, it would have no
authority to enforce its advice.

When a facility actually underwent a major cut in
defense work, the ready conversion plan would be put into
effect. Workers would be retrained for civilian operation.
During the period of changeover, they would be eligible for
income support equal to 90% of the first $20,000 and 50% of
the next $5,000 of their previous income and continuation of
medical coverage, pension and other benefits for up to two
years. Those who could not be employed at the converted
facility would also be given re-employment assistance and
relocation allowances. The money to finance worker benefits
would come from a pooled fund into which every defense contractor would be required to pay 1.25% of its total military
contract value. (The tax is on revenue rather than profit
to avoid accounting manipulation of profit figures.) As a
rough estimate, the entire economic conversion process can
be expected to take from two to four years. It will involve
a great deal of detailed planning (mostly on a local basis)
and careful implementation, at the cost of a considerable
investment of time and effort. However, the economic and
social benefits which will accrue as a result of this
investment are truly enormous.

The evidence of the failure of present economic policies
is ubiquitous. The progressive weakening of the domestic and
international strength of the U.S. and its influence as a
world nation cannot be reversed until the nation discards
the illusory pursuit of strength and influence through military expansionism for the hard realities of economic redevelopment. And this can only come via the conversion process.

Appendix A

The Defense Economic Adjustment Act

(S. 2279, November 2, 1977)

Be it enacted by the Senate and House of Representatives of the United States of America in Congress assembled, That this Act may be cited as the "Defense Economic Adjustment Act."

DECLARATION OF PURPOSE AND POLICY

SEC. 2. (a) The Congress finds and declares that the United States during the past two and one-half decades made heavy economic, scientific, and technical commitments for defense; that these commitments led to the development of specialized skills and business practices not directly applicable in the civilian sector of the economy; that as these commitments are modified to take account of changing requirements for national security and domestic needs, careful preparation is necessary if serious economic dislocations are to be avoided; and that the economic ability of the Nation and of management, labor, and capital to adjust to changing security needs is consistent with the general welfare of the United States.

(b) It is the purpose of this Act to provide the means through which the United States can promote orderly economic adjustment which will (1) minimize the dislocation of workers, communities, and industries, (2) assure that the dislocations do not compound recessionary trends, and (3) encourage conversion of technologies and managerial and worker skills developed in defense production to the service of projects in the civilian sector.

DEFINITIONS

SEC. 3. As used in this Act, the term--

(1) "Council" means the Defense Economic Adjustment Council established under section 101 of this Act.

(2) "Defense agency" means the Department of Defense, the Energy Research and Development Administration, or the National Aeronautics and Space Administration.

(3) "Defense contract" means any contract entered into between a person or non-profit organization and a defense agency to furnish defense material or services to such

agency, and any contract entered into between a person or nonprofit organization and any foreign country or person acting on behalf of a foreign country to furnish defense material or services to or for such country pursuant to the Arms Export Control Act, or similar Act.

(4) "Defense contractor" means any person having not less than five per centum of the organization's labor force engaged in the furnishing of defense material pursuant to the terms of the defense contract or subcontract and for whom such contract or contracts, including any under negotiation, represents more than 20 per centum of the total plant business.

(5) "Defense facility" means any private plant or other establishment (or part thereof) used under a defense contract or engaged in the production, repair, modification, maintenance, storage, or handling of defense material, or any Government-owned military facility such as a base, fort, shipyard, or depot.

(6) "Defense material" means any item of weaponry, munitions, equipment, or specialized supplies or services intended for use by a defense agency or for sale to or for the use of a foreign country which has primarily military application.

(7) "Defense service" means the research, development, production, test, inspection, or repair of any defense material for use by a defense agency or pursuant to a defense contract.

(8) "Displaced" or "displacement" means with respect to any worker of a defense facility or defense agency the separation, on a permanent or temporary basis, of such worker from employment with such facility or agency.

(9) "Fund" means the Workers Economic Adjustment Reserve Trust Fund established by title III of this Act.

(10) "Person" means any corporation, firm, partnership, association, individual, or other entity.

(11) "State" includes the District of Columbia and the Commonwealth of Puerto Rico.

(12) "State agency" means the agency of a State which administers its unemployment compensation law, approved by the Secretary of Labor under section 3304 of the Internal Revenue Code of 1954.

(13) "Substantially and seriously affected" means any community in which more than 5 per centum of its labor force is directly employed by a defense facility or contractor in furnishing specialized materials or services under a defense contract.

TITLE I--DEFENSE ECONOMIC ADJUSTMENT COUNCIL ESTABLISHMENT

SEC. 101. (a) There is established in the Executive Office of the President the Defense Economic Adjustment Council which shall be composed of--

    (1) the Secretary of Commerce;
    (2) the Secretary of Labor;
    (3) the Secretary of Health, Education, and Welfare;
    (4) the Secretary of Housing and Urban Development;
    (5) the Secretary of Transportation;
    (6) the Chairman of the Council of Economic Advisors;
    (7) six representatives of the business-management community who represent nondefense business to be appointed by the President; and
    (8) six representatives of labor union organizations to be appointed by the President.

    (b) The Secretary of Commerce shall be Chairman of the Council, shall preside over meetings of the Council and shall designate a member of the Council to preside in the absence of the Chairman.

    (c) (1) An Office of Economic Adjustment shall be established within the Executive Office of the President to provide staff support for the Council with a maximum staff size of fifteen. The Office shall be headed by an Executive Secretary who shall be appointed by the President (after consultation with the Council) and who shall be compensated at the rate provided for grade 18 of the General Schedule under section 5332 of title 5, United States Code.
    (2) The members of such staff and any task force established by the Council shall include marketing specialists, production engineers, plant layout experts, urban planning experts, and manpower training experts. At the request of the Council, the staff and any task force established by the Council shall carry out such duties as the Council may prescribe.
    (3) The Council may appoint and fix the compensation of such personnel as it deems advisable. The Council may procure temporary and intermittent services to the same extent as authorized by section 3109 of title 5, United States Code.

(4)   The Council is authorized to secure directly from any executive department, bureau, agency, board, commission, office, independent establishment, or instrumentality, information, suggestions, estimates, and statistics to carry out the Act, and each such entity shall furnish such information, suggestions, estimates, and statistics directly to the Council upon request made by the Chairman.

(d)   Members of the Council who are officers or employees of the Federal Government shall receive no additional compensation by virtue of membership on the Council. Other members appointed to the Council shall receive compensation at the rate of not to exceed $135 per diem when engaged in the performance of duties of the Council. While away from their homes or regular places of business in the performance of services for the Council, members of the Council shall be allowed travel expenses, including per diem in lieu of subsistence, in the same manner as persons employed intermittently in the Government service are allowed expenses under section 5703(b) of title 5, United States Code.

DUTIES

SEC. 102   (a)   The Council shall—

(1)   encourage the preparation of concrete plans for civilian-oriented public projects addressing vital areas of national concern (such as mass transportation, housing, education, health care, environmental protection, renewable energy resources, etc.) by the various civilian agencies of the Federal Government, as well as by State and local governments;

(2)   supervise the establishment in the Department of Labor of a Job Information Bank intended to coordinate State, local and Federal employment services so as to serve as a resource on civilian job information for workers released from defense-related employment as a result of the shifting or reduction, or both, of defense-related expenditures;

(3)   prepare suggestive lists, by geographic region and area of specialization, for organizations and individual consultants in fields such as marketing, facilities design, organization, production engineering, and engineering economy whose major professional experience has been in civilian-oriented activity, and furnish such lists to local Alternative Use Committees upon their request, without explicit or implicit endorsement of the personnel so listed;

(4)   prepare and distribute a Conversion Guidelines Handbook, not to exceed 300 pages in length, which shall—

(A)   include a discussion of the basic problems
involved in the retraining, reorientation and reorganization
of personnel (managerial, technical, administrative and production) and the redirection of physical plants for efficient, civilian-oriented productive activity;

(B)   outline the basic requirements of programs for
professional retraining of managerial personnel in order to
reorient them to the management of civilian, market-oriented
enterprise;

(C)   outline the basic requirements for a program
of professional retraining of technical personnel in order
to effectively re-orient them to the prevailing conditions
of research, product design and production operations within
civilian-oriented facilities;

(D)   outline the basic requirements for the length
and nature of occupational retraining for production workers
and junior level administrative employees;

(E)   include illustrative case studies of successful conversion to efficient civilian-oriented production, or
references thereto;

(F)   provide a checklist of critical points requiring attention at each stage of the conversion process;

(G)   contain an annotated bibliography of
conversion related works; and

(H)   be revised, as necessary, every two years;
and

(5)   perform such other duties as are imposed upon the
Council by this Act; and

(6)   promulgate such regulations as may be necessary to
carry out the provisions of this Act.

TITLE II--ALTERNATIVE USE
COMMITTEES ESTABLISHMENT

SEC. 201   (a)   There shall be established at every defense
facility employing at least 200 persons, and at every
business concern having at least 20 per centum of gross
revenue due to business resulting from any defense contract
or contracts, an Alternative Use Committee to undertake
economic conversion planning and preparation for the employment of the personnel and utilization of the facilities in
the event of a reduction or elimination of any defense
facility or the curtailment, conclusion or disapproval of
any defense contract, resulting in substantial and serious
unemployment.

(b)   In the case of a defense facility that is a
Government military installation, the Alternative Use
Committee shall consist of at least nine members, an equal
number of whom shall (1) be designated by the base commander,
(2) represent the civilian employees of the installation,

and (3) represent the local community and interested citizens as designated by the chief executive officer of the local government of the community, but shall not include any individuals employed at the military installation.

(c)   (1)   In the case of a defense facility that is not a governmental military installation, and of any defense contractor subject to subsection (a), there shall be included in each defense contract provisions to assure that an Alternative Use Committee is established in accordance with the provisions of this subsection.

(2)   The Alternative Use Committees shall consist of at least nine members, an equal number of whom shall be named by--

(A)   the management of the facility,

(B)   the non-management employees of the facility, and

(C)   the chief executive officer of the local community government, representing the local community, interested citizens, but shall not include any individuals employed at the defense facility.

(d)   The Funds for performing the planning and reporting requirements imposed under this title as applied to defense contractors, including market research, independent studies and the employment of specialized personnel, shall be paid from funds derived from the military contract or base operating costs at a rate equal to $50 per employee per year in the first year and $25 per employee per year in subsequent years.   Office space shall also be provided by the management of the facility, without charge.

FUNCTIONS OF THE ALTERNATIVE
USE COMMITTEES

SEC. 202   (a)   The Alternative Use Committee shall--

(1)   evaluate the assets of the defense facility and the resources and requirements of the local community in terms of physical property, manpower skills and expertise, accessibility, environment, and economic needs;

(2)   develop and review at least once every two years detailed plans for the conversion of the facility to efficient, civilian-oriented productive activity to be carried out in the event the facility is substantially and seriously affected by a government decision to reduce, modify, or close the facility, conclude any defense contracts, or disapprove a license to sell or export defense materials to non-government parties;

(3)   provide occupational retraining and re-employment counseling services for all employees to be displaced by the implementation of a conversion plan or closing of the

facility, beginning 18 months before the date of commence-
ment of the implementation of that plan or the permanent
closing of that facility; and

(4) dissolve itself and return all of its assets to
the control of the management of the facility immediately
upon final completion of the conversion process.

ADMINISTRATIVE PROVISIONS

SEC. 203 (a) The Alternative Use Committees may hire staff
personnel as well as any specialists it may determine
necessary.

(b) The Alternative Use Committees are authorized to
obtain a complete and detailed inventory of all land, buildings, capital equipment and other equipment, including its
condition, and are authorized to obtain information regarding the occupations and skills of all civilian employees of
the facility.

CONVERSION PLANS

SEC. 204 (a) The conversion plans shall--

(1) be so designed as to maximize the extent to which
the personnel required for the efficient operation of the
converted facility can be drawn from personnel with the
types and levels of skill approximating skills levels and
types possessed by civilian personnel employed at the
defense facility prior to its conversion;

(2) specify the numbers of civilian personnel, by type
and level of skill, employed at the facility prior to conversion, whose continued employment is not consistent with
efficient operation of the civilian-oriented converted
facility;

(3) specify the numbers of positions, by level and
type of skill, if any, that will be needed at the converted
facility because personnel employed at the pre-converted
facility do not possess the levels or types of skills
required;

(4) indicate in detail what new plant and equipment
and modifications to existing plant and equipment are required for the converted facility;

(5) include an estimate of financing requirements and
a financial plan for the conversion; and

(6) provide for completion of the entire conversion
process within a period not to exceed 2 years.

TITLE III--ECONOMIC ADJUSTMENT
FUND ESTABLISHED

SEC. 301   There is hereby established in the Treasury of

the United States a trust fund to be known as the "Workers
Economic Adjustment   Reserve Trust Fund."

DEPOSITS INTO THE FUND

SEC. 302 (a) The Federal Government shall not enter into
any defense contract with any defense contractor to furnish
defense material or services to a defense agency, nor shall
it permit the sale of such defense material or services to
or on behalf of any other country, unless the defense contractor fulfills a requirement to pay to the Fund an amount
equal to one and a quarter percent per year of the value of
the contractor's gross revenue on such sales.

   (b) Amounts paid by a defense contractor pursuant to
this section shall be deposited in the Fund.

MANAGEMENT OF THE FUND

SEC. 303 (a) It shall be the duty of the Secretary of the
Treasury to invest such portion of the moneys in the Fund as
is not, in the judgment of the Secretary, required to meet
current withdrawal requirements. Such investments may be
made only in interest-bearing obligations of the United
States or in obligations guaranteed as to both principal and
interest by the United States. For such purpose, such obligations may be acquired (1) on original issue at the issue
price, or (2) by purchase of outstanding obligations at the
market price. The purposes for which obligations of the
United States may be issued under the Second Liberty Bond
Act, as amended, are hereby extended to authorize the
issuance at par of special obligations exclusively to the
Fund. Such special obligations shall bear interest at a
rate equal to the average rate of interest, computed as to
the end of the calendar month next preceding the date of
such issue, borne by all marketable interest-bearing obligations of the United States then forming part of the public
debt; except that where such average rate is not a multiple
of one-eighth of 1 per centum, the rate of interest of such
special obligations shall be the multiple of one-eighth of
1 per centum next lower than such average rate. Such obligations shall be issued only if the Secretary of the
Treasury determines that the purchase of other interest-
bearing obligations of the United States, or of obligations
guaranteed as to both principal and interest by the United
States on original issue or at the market place, is not in
the public interest.

   (b) Any obligation acquired by the Fund (except
special obligations issued exclusively to the Fund) may be
sold by the Secretary of the Treasury at the market price,

and such special obligations may be reduced at par plus
accrued interest.

TITLE IV--ECONOMIC ADJUSTMENT ASSISTANCE
FOR WORKERS CERTIFICATION

SEC. 401 (a) All displacements affecting more than 5 per
centum of workers employed by a defense contractor attributable, in whole or in part, to a reduction of the volume of
defense work in such facility shall upon certification by
the local Alternative Use Committee be reported by the management of the firm or government facility to the State
employment office acting as Agent for the administration of
the employees benefit program.

(b) Any worker (or union representing such worker) of
a defense contractor in a report filed by such contractor
pursuant to subsection (a) of this section (or by any
matter relating to such worker's certification, or failure
to be so certified, or such worker's eligibility for such
conversion benefits, or the kind or amount thereof), shall
be entitled to appeal such matter to the Secretary of Labor,
or, if such worker is in a State which has entered into a
contract with the Council pursuant to section 403 of this
Act, to the appropriate State agency.

ENTITLEMENT TO BENEFITS

SEC. 402 (a) Any worker certified pursuant to section 401
of this Act as eligible for adjustment benefits by reason
of such worker's displacement from a defense contractor shall
be entitled, for the two-year period following displacement,
to whichever of the following benefits are applicable:

(1) Compensation, on a weekly basis, sufficient, when
added to any benefits which such worker receives or is
entitled to receive for such weekly period under any Federal
or State unemployment compensation program (or any plan of
such worker's employer providing for such benefits) by
reason of such worker's displacement, and any earnings during
such weekly period from other employment, to maintain an
income at a level equal to 90 per centum of the first
$20,000 per year and 50 per centum of the next $5,000 in
excess of $20,000 for that year of that worker's regular
annual wages (based on a forty-hour workweek, or, in the
event a defense contractor has a regular workweek payable at
straight-time wage rates other than forty hours, for such
regular workweek) prior to that worker's displacement.

(2) Vested pension credit under any applicable pension

plan maintained by the defense contractor from which such worker was displaced, for the period of that worker's employment with such facility, and the two-year period following that worker's displacement, during which two-year, for the purpose of the Employment Retirement Income Security Act of 1974 and the corresponding provisions of the Internal Revenue Code of 1954 (relating to a qualified plan) such worker shall be treated as if such worker were employed by such contractor on the same basis as such worker was employed on the day preceding such worker's displacement; except that pension credit during such two-year period shall be reduced to the extent of vested pension credit earned with another employer during such two-year period.

(3) Maintenance of any hospital, surgical, medical, disability, life (and other survivor) insurance coverage which such individual (including members of such individual's family) had by reason of employment by a defense contractor prior to such displacement; except that if such worker so displaced is otherwise employed during such two-year period, such worker shall be entitled to receive benefits under this paragraph to the extent necessary to provide such worker with the same protection described in this paragraph as such worker (including family members) would have had if such worker had not been displaced.

(4) Retraining for civilian work providing pay and status as comparable as possible to the employment from which such worker was displaced or retraining under titles I, II, or III of the Comprehensive Employment and Training Act of 1973.

(5) Retraining for civilian work, approved by the Secretary of Labor or, in the case of a worker in a State which has entered into a contract with the Council pursuant to section 403 of this Act, by the State agency, and reimbursement for all reasonable relocation expenses as specified in regulations prescribed by the Secretary of Labor incurred by such worker in moving to another location in order to take advantage of an employment opportunity to which such worker is referred, or which is determined to be suitable, by the Secretary of Labor or, the case of a worker in a State which has entered into a contract with the Council pursuant to section 403 of this Act, by the State agency.

(6) No individual shall be eligible for more than one conversion related program of benefits.

(b) All managerial and technical employees who have spent more than 50 per centum of the ten years preceding

implementation of the conversion plan working in defense-
related industry or at military bases must participate in or
have completed a program of professional retraining meeting
the requirements specified in the Conversion Guidelines
Handbook of the Defense Economic Adjustment Council in order
to be eligible for the special financial assistance, relocation aid and special job information services provided by
this Act. All other employees may elect to enter such a
program.

STATE AGREEMENTS

SEC. 403 (a) The Council is authorized to enter and shall,
on behalf of the United States, enter into an agreement with
a State, or with any agency administering the unemployment
compensation law of any State approved by the Secretary of
Labor under section 3304 of the Internal Revenue Code of
1954, which--

(1) as agent of the Council, shall upon certifications
and other determinations required in section 401 of this Act,
make such payments and provide such benefits as are authorized by section 402 of this Act, on the basis provided for
in this Act, and shall otherwise cooperate with the Council
and other State agencies in carrying out the provisions of
this Act; and

(2) shall be reimbursed for all benefits paid pursuant
to such agreement and all administrative costs incurred in
carrying out such agreement.

(b) (1) There shall be paid to each State agency which
has an agreement under this section, either in advance or by
way of reimbursement, as may be determined by the Council,
such sum as the Council estimates the agency will be entitled
to receive under such agreement for each calendar month,
reduced or increased, as the case may be, by any sum by which
the Council finds that its estimates for any prior calendar
month were greater or less than amounts which should have
been paid to the agency. Such estimates may be made upon
the basis of statistical sampling, or other method as agreed
upon by the Council and the State agency.

(2) The Council shall from time to time certify to
the Secretary of the Treasury for payment to each State
agency which has an agreement under this section sums payable
to such agency under paragraph (1) of this subsection. The
Secretary of the Treasury, prior to audit or settlement by
the General Accounting Office, shall make payments to the
agency, in accordance with such certification, from the Fund.

(3) All money paid a State agency under any such
agreement shall be used solely for the purposes for which it
is paid; and any money so paid which is not used for such
purposes shall be returned, at the time specified in such
agreement, to the Treasury.

(c) In any case involving a worker entitled to benefits
under section 402 who is in a State with respect to which
there is no agreement pursuant to this section, the Secretary
of Labor shall, under regulations prescribed by the Secretary,
administer such benefits on behalf of such worker. The
Secretary of Labor, in administering such benefits, shall,
from time to time, certify to the Secretary of the Treasury
for payment to such worker the amounts of such benefits to
which such worker is entitled, and the Secretary of the
Treasury shall make payments to such worker, in accordance
with such certification, from the Fund.

LIMITATION ON BENEFITS

SEC. 404. In no case shall any displaced worker be eligible
for benefits under section 402(a) of this Act unless such
worker agrees (1) to maintain, on a current basis, during
the period of his displacement, an active registration with
the Secretary of Labor or an appropriate State employment
agency, as the case may be, and (2) to accept any employment,
determined by the Secretary of Labor or agency, as the case
may be, to be suitable, to which such worker is referred by
the Secretary of Labor or such agency. No such benefits
shall be paid under this Act to any worker who fails to maintain such registration or to accept such employment.

TREATMENT OF UNEMPLOYMENT COMPENSATION

SEC. 405. In no case shall any adjustment benefits paid
pursuant to this Act be taken into consideration in determining eligibility for unemployment compensation under any
Federal or State unemployment compensation law or in determining the amount of entitlement thereunder.

TERMINATION OF BENEFITS

SEC. 406. Adjustment benefits shall terminate when a worker
eligible for benefits obtains employment providing 90 per
centum of the first $20,000 per year and 50 per centum of the
next $5,000 in excess of $20,000 for that year of that
worker's previous wages or two years after displacement,
whichever occurs sooner.

TITLE V--USE OF CERTAIN
RESEARCH FUNDS
AMENDMENT TO PUBLIC LAW 91-441

SEC. 501.   (a) Section 203(a) of the Act of October 7, 1970 (Public Law 91-441) is amended by--

(1)   inserting "or, in the opinion of the Defense Economic Adjustment Council, a potential relationship to an urgent national requirement in a designated nondefense sector," after "function of operation";

(2)   inserting "or the Defense Economic Adjustment Council" after "Department of Defense" in paragraph (1); and

(3)   adding at the end of such section 203 the following: "(f)   The Defense Economic Adjustment Council shall be required to define urgent national requirements for nondefense sectors of the economy, and shall be required to include in the designation, any areas so defined by the Congress.   Research and development related to energy and fuel efficiency shall be considered a designated area."

(b)   Section 204 of such Act is amended by inserting "or, in the opinion of the Defense Economic Adjustment Council, a potential relationship to an urgent national requirement in a designated nondefense sector of the economy" after "military function or operation."

TITLE VI--AUTHORIZATION
OF APPROPRIATIONS

APPROPRIATIONS AUTHORIZED

SEC. 601.   There are authorized to be appropriated such sums as may be necessary to carry out the provisions of this Act.

DEFENSE ECONOMIC ADJUSTMENT ACT
(Summary of Provisions)

I.   PURPOSE

To provide advance planning for effective conversion of defense-related industries to productive civilian activity, and to provide economic adjustment assistance to affected communities, industries, and workers which may be substantially and seriously affected by reductions in defense expenditures.

II. DEFINITIONS

Defines terms used in bill. Defines "substantially and seriously affected" for communities and contractors, so that bill covers those who would be hardest hit by reductions in defense expenditures and would have the most difficulty in adjusting.

III. TITLE I--ESTABLISHMENT OF COUNCIL

SEC. 101: Establishes a Defense Economic Adjustment Council in the Executive Office of the President, membership to include Cabinet officers, representatives of business-management community, and representatives of labor union organizations. The Secretary of Commerce is Chairman.

SEC. 102: Defines duties of Council as follows: encouraging preparation of plans for civilian-oriented public projects addressing vital areas of national concern; supervising establishment of Job Information Bank in Department of Labor to coordinate State, local and Federal employment services; preparing lists of organizations and consultants engaged in civilian-oriented activity for use by local conversion committees; and preparing and distributing a Conversion Guidelines Handbook.

IV. TITLE II--ESTABLISHMENT OF ALTERNATIVE USE COMMITTEES

SEC. 201: Establishes local Alternative Use Committees to undertake economic conversion planning and preparation for employment of personnel and utilization of facilities in the event of reductions in defense spending resulting in substantial and serious unemployment; and provides a fund for performing these duties to be derived from the military contract or base operating costs.

SEC. 202: Describes functions of Alternative Use Committees: evaluating assets of defense facility and resources and requirements of local community; developing and reviewing plans for conversion to civilian-oriented productive activity; and providing occupational retraining and counseling services for displaced employees.

SEC. 203: Authorizes the Alternative Use Committee to hire staff personnel; to obtain an inventory of all land and equipment, including its condition; and to obtain information regarding the occupations and skills of all civilian employees of the facility.

SEC. 204:   Requires that conversion plans be designed to
most efficiently use civilian personnel employed at the
facility prior to conversion; requires detailed listing of
any new plant and equipment and modification to existing
equipment needed for conversion; requires an estimate of
financing requirements and financial plan for conversion;
and provides for completion of entire conversion process
within a period not to exceed two years.

V.   TITLE III--ESTABLISHMENT OF ECONOMIC ADJUSTMENT FUND

SEC. 301:   Provides for establishment in Treasury of a trust
fund to be known as the "Workers Economic Adjustment Reserve
Trust Fund."

SEC. 302:   Requires defense contractors to pay to the Fund
an amount equal to one and a quarter percent per year of
their gross revenue.

SEC. 303:   Requires the Secretary of the Treasury to invest
that portion of the Fund not required to meet current
withdrawals.

VI.   TITLE IV--ECONOMIC ADJUSTMENT ASSISTANCE FOR WORKERS

SEC. 401:   Requires that all displacements affecting more
than five percent of the workers be reported to the State
employment office or agency acting as Agent for administration of employees' benefits programs.

SEC. 402:   Provides eligible workers with two year entitlement to applicable benefits: compensation on a weekly basis
to maintain an income equal to ninety percent of the first
$20,000 per year and fifty percent of the next $5,000 in
excess of $20,000; vested pension credit; maintenance of
hospital, surgical, medical, disability, and life insurance
coverage; retraining for civilian work; and necessary relocation expenses.   Requires all managerial and technical
employees who have spent more than fifty percent of the ten
years preceding implementation of the plan to participate in
a professional retraining program in order to be eligible for
benefits.

SEC. 403:   Authorizes the Council to reimburse a State or
administering agency (acting as agent of the Council) for all
benefits paid.

VII.   TITLE V--USE OF CERTAIN RESEARCH FUNDS

SEC. 501:   Amends Defense Authorization Act of 1970 to
expand kinds of independent research and development which
can be funded in a defense contract to include projects
which the Council believes have a potential relationship to
an urgent national requirement in a designated nondefense
sector.   Council and Congress permitted to designate nondefense R & D which can be funded.

VIII.   TITLE VI

Authorizes appropriation of sums which may be necessary
to carry out provisions of this Act.

Appendix B

Questions and Answers About Economic Conversion
and the Defense Economic Adjustment Act

Conversion: The Broader Issues

(1) Why conversion? Why not diversification?
Defense firms can protect themselves against the fluctuations
in defense contracting by buying other nondefense businesses,
so that profits can be kept up even if defense contracts are
lost. But this financial protection for the firms does not
protect the jobs of the workers in the defense plants owned
by that company, nor does it protect the economy of the
communities in which the defense plants are located. Only
planning for conversion, i.e., for alternate civilian activity at those plants, will give the workers and communities
this kind of economic security in the event of severe cutbacks in defense activity at their local plant or military
base.

(2) Isn't it unnecessary to plan for conversion unless
there will be major cuts in the military budget?
Planning for conversion is important even in a situation of
a _growing_ military budget, because there are always shifts
of contracts and base closings. For example, although the
military budget is presently expanding, the cancellation of
the B-1 bomber program, the closing of the Frankford Arsenal,
the loss of helicopter contracts by Boeing Vertol have
thrown thousands of employees out of work because there are
no standby plans for alternative work for them to do. But,
of course, cutting the military budget would make the need
for conversion plans much greater. Knowing that ready plans
are always available to prevent job loss and other temporary
economic problems related to military cutbacks will also make
it easier to remove this militarily irrelevant question from
the debate on whether or not any proposed military program
is required for national security purposes.

(3) Isn't it easier just to keep military contracts flowing
to all military firms?
Military decisions should be made for military national
security reasons. The Congress and the President should not
feel compelled to build what is not needed for national
security purposes just to keep defense workers employed.
Such compulsion is not in the best interests of the military
or of the nation's security. Beyond this, even Adam Smith,
the father of capitalism, writing in the Wealth of Nations
in 1776, stressed that military spending was a burden on the
economy. Recent economic trends give credence to the idea

that persistent, high military spending drains the civilian
economy, adversely affecting the competitiveness of industry.
As U.S. industries have become less competitive, foreign and
domestic markets have been lost, with major unemployment-
generating effects. Furthermore, military spending has been
shown to create fewer jobs dollar for dollar than nearly
all other forms of government spending or an equivalent tax
cut. Thus, job opportunities are lost in this way too.
Clearly, the nation's economy should not be subjected to
this kind of strain more than is strictly required for the
legitimate purposes of national defense.

(4) Why should a conversion bill focus on military industry
alone? What about the problems of dislocations in the steel
industry, in textiles, clothing and elsewhere?
Military industry and bases are a clear and immediate area
of government responsibility. The resources (especially
labor) employed in military activity are there directly
because of federal government funding decisions. The defense agencies are their only customer. Since it was government spending patterns that drew them into this area and it
will be changes in government spending patterns that push
them out, the federal responsibility for assuring a smooth
transfer is obvious and indisputable. This is not true of
any private civilian industry. Besides this, the problem of
handling the transfer of resources (especially people)
smoothly and effectively from the world of military activity
to the very different world of civilian activity is qualita-
tively different from the problem of facilitating the
transfer of resources within the civilian economy. Therefore,
it is best not to try to address both problems with the same
legislated mechanism. However, it should be noted that
nothing in the idea or the mechanics of effective conversion
planning prejudices in any way the case for broader economic
dislocation adjustment.

(5) Why shouldn't the problem of economic conversion be
handled by (or possibly an expanded version of) the already
existing Office of Economic Adjustment of the Department of
Defense?
To begin with, it would seem clearly in the best interests
of the nation that the Department of Defense devote its full
and complete attention to military matters--this is its
mandate, its raison d'etre. It should not have its attention diverted from this central function by any other
considerations. If decisions made with respect to the
purchase of weapons and allied systems, the structure of
forces, logistical considerations, etc. produce the need to
transfer resources to alternate civilian activity to prevent
economic dislocation, it may be obvious that the government's

responsibility for smoothing the transition is compelling,
but it is also obvious that responsibility should not lie
with the military. To the extent that there is federal involvement in what is essentially the socio-economic activity
of conversion, it should be through agencies such as the
Department of Commerce and Labor, the Council of Economic
Advisors, etc. whose responsibilities are in this area.
Furthermore, there are about 20,000 major military industry
contractors and about 400 military bases of size. To ask a
single federal group to be responsible for the detailed
development or even the detailed review and evaluation of so
many alternate use plans, plans that would be continually
modified and updated as changing economic conditions shift
potential markets, is unwise if not completely infeasible.
In addition to creating a huge new bureaucracy, undesirable
in its own right, it is extremely unlikely that such a complex, dynamic and diverse task could be effectively performed
in this way.

The Defense Economic Adjustment Act

(1) Why is the main planning responsibility and authority
placed in the hands of a <u>local</u> Alternate Use Committee,
rather than a central, federal agency?
Because of the huge number of major military contractors
(20,000) and large bases (400) in the U.S., an attempt to do
detailed plant-by-plant and base-by-base conversion planning,
or plan evaluation, from a centralized office is almost
certain to be ineffective. To be workable, each conversion
plan must be tailored to the specifics of the facility for
which it is made. This requires the sort of detailed knowledge of labor force and capital equipment, plant site
advantages and disadvantages and even economic characteristics of the surrounding community that is most effectively
obtained by those who know the facility and the area best--
those who work and live there. In addition, the employees,
local management and local community people have the
greatest vested interest in making sure the standby plan will
work if put into effect. They clearly have far more to lose
from its failure (or gain from its success) than any distant
planning expert, no matter how well intentioned. Finally,
if the local committees feel the need for expert technical
assistance in their planning, they not only have full
authority to hire consultants from the planning funds they
are given, but have access to an informational list of
qualified local consultants provided under the bill's mandate by the National Economic Adjustment Council.

(2) Why a three-part local committee? Why not leave the
planning up to the management?

Because of management's ability to protect itself financially through diversification, a prospect that still leaves workers and the local communities vulnerable, it is unwise to leave planning for conversion in their hands alone. The purpose of a tri-partite structure is to bring together all three parties at interest in a setting that prevents any one of them from roadblocking. It is clear that though labor, management and the community all have a major stake in having input into the planning process, they each have a different point of view and different particular interests. There is real value in the interactive process that will result from the alternate use committees mandate to produce a unified plan.

(3) How do we know the plans will be well done and workable? There is no way to guarantee that the plans will work, but giving the people most affected by the success or failure of the plan the responsibility and authority for drawing it up makes it highly likely that it will be done seriously and well. Self interest is a powerful motivator. Direct federal oversight, evaluation and certification of plans is simply unworkable, for reasons discussed earlier under the question of local vs. central planning. It is also not clear that such oversight would improve plan quality.

(4) Why isn't the Department of Defense (DOD) at the head of the national council?
The DOD's organizational mandate is to deal with military problems. Conversion is not a military problem, it is an economic, business/labor problem, and such problems do not properly fall within the purview of the DOD, but rather that of federal agencies such as the Departments of Commerce and Labor.

(5) What if a facility can't be converted?
It will most likely be an extremely rare event that no feasible civilian alternative can be found for a given military facility. What is more likely, in fact nearly certain, is that some types of workers employed at any given military facility will not be employed at an efficient civilian version of that facility. This is particularly true of engineers and scientists who are presently in military industry firms in concentrations far greater than is consistent with any civilian alternative. But that is precisely why this bill provides for a "people-oriented" rather than a "facility oriented" conversion process. Provisions are made for relocation aid, job placement assistance, retraining, etc. so that all civilian employees of the military facility are assisted in their personal job conversion, whether or not they will be employable at the converted facility. Note,

though, that the alternate use committees are instructed to
develop a plan which minimizes this kind of relocation
(within the context of efficient civilian operation).

(6) What advantage does conversion have for the firms? Why
aren't they given federal financing, tax incentives, etc. to
encourage conversion?
If there is a severe cutback or total halt in defense-
related activity at a given facility, activating the ready
conversion plan allows the firm to earn money at a facility
that would otherwise not be generating any revenue. There is
a real problem in providing incentives for conversion because
it is difficult to justify a governmental subsidy to a
former military plant which would give it a competitive
advantage over existing, already civilian, firms not receiving such subsidy. The bill does provide for temporary
worker subsidies for retraining which, in effect, subsidizes
the firm indirectly by giving it a labor force that can
function effectively in a civilian enterprise. This should
put the converting firm on a roughly equal footing with
competing civilian firms without giving it an unfair
advantage.

(7) Where will the new markets for the products of converted
facilities come from?
The national council is mandated to direct each of the
civilian departments of the federal government to draw up a
ranked list of concrete and specific projects that they
would fund if they received additional monies as a result of
changed federal budget priorities. These lists are made into
a master list of civilian government funding priorities
(which could also include tax cuts) and funds to be returned
to state and local governments that would also be made
available to the alternate use committees. Because these
lists are in order of priority, the committees would have a
clear idea of what markets are likely to come into being
when money is shifted from the military, and hence could
build at least part of their plan around these potential
markets.

(8) What is to prevent all the alternative use committees
from planning for the same civilian products unless there is
some sort of central plan coordination?
There is no unique product to which the attention of any
given facility can be turned. It is nearly always possible
to come up with a number of different products, serving
different markets, that are possible alternatives. Such
diversified planning will be encouraged by the guidelines in
the handbook prepared by the national council. If each
alternate use committee develops multiple plans, the

likelihood that a large number of facilities converting at
once would all choose the same particular product from their
planned options seems remote. As some facilities convert,
they may saturate a particular product area, but since planning is an ongoing process, all that would mean is that the
committees at unconverted facilities would drop that product
from their own plans.

(9) Isn't this bill going to generate a huge new government
bureaucracy?
At the federal level, a statutory maximum of 15 new staff
people would be hired. Maximum use is made of existing
state agencies to administer worker adjustment benefits so
as to avoid generating bureaucracy. Decentralized planning
will also eliminate the need for a large new government
apparatus. The bill is strongly oriented to minimize
central government administration.

(10) Why do planning at all facilities in advance? Why not
do plans as the government decides to cancel military
programs or close bases?
Widespread advance planning is extremely important for two
main reasons. First, lead time (i.e., time in advance of
contract cancellation or base closure) is required for
effective conversion planning, yet the DOD itself might not
know which of two competing weapons systems it will fund,
for example, until the "last minute" when prototypes are
tested. If all facilities have plans ready in advance, this
problem is greatly mitigated, if not solved. Second, if
planning is done a piece at a time, as contracts are cut or
bases are closed, there will be more uncertainty about the
ability to deal with a particular economic dislocation than
if developed plans are known to exist. Thus, Congress and
the President will feel more pressured by the jobs issue in
deciding on given military programs, rather than being able
to devote full attention to what should be the only consider-
ation--the merits of the weapons system as a contributor to
national security.

(11) What if the company decides to shut the facility down
and leave rather than implement the conversion plan?
Provision should be made for purchase of the facility by the
workers and/or the community and/or a civilian company who
would then implement the plan themselves. In the first two
cases, federal financial assistance should be made available
if required, in the form of loan guarantees or mortgage
loans. It should be noted that this is only a potential
problem where a private defense contractor owns the facility
--military bases and government-owned production facilities

whether operated by a private firm or by the government
present no particular difficulty.

(12) What will it cost the taxpayer to do all this planning
and ultimately provide worker adjustment benefits?
The planning is relatively inexpensive. At $50.00 per
civilian employee, the cost would be roughly $50 million for
all defense base employees and $95 million for all defense
industry employees. The workers benefits are financed out
of the contract at the rate of 1.25% of revenues, which
amounts to $402 million for 1978, assuming 1978 defense pro-
curement of $32,200 million. However, these monies do not
come from the taxpayers--they are taken from the contractors.
Perhaps just as important is what it costs not to do this
sort of advanced planning, in terms of lost income for laid-
off workers and those who sell goods and services to them,
and lost tax revenues resulting from idle facilities and
unemployed workers, not to mention the tax drain of unemployment insurance.

References

1. <u>New York Times</u> (July 27, 1972)

2. In fact, if the equipment and/or the personnel operat-
    ing it perform poorly, this can often be blatantly
    turned into an argument for further increases in the
    military budget, as for example was the case in the
    aftermath of the failed attempt to rescue the U.S.
    hostages held in Iran in 1980. If the military had had
    even more money, the argument went, it could afford to
    buy equipment that would perform better!

3. Finney, John W. "C5A Jet Repairs to Cost $1.5 Billion,"
    <u>New York Times</u> (December 5, 1975).

4. Melman, Seymour, <u>The Permanent War Economy</u> (New York:
    Simon and Shuster, 1974), p. 85.

5. Op. Cit., John W. Finney.

6. "Bart in Transit," <u>Newsweek</u> (January 12, 1976).

7. Ibid.

8. <u>The New York Post</u> (December 15, 1971).

9. Anderson, J.R., <u>The Impact of the Pentagon Tax on U.S.
    Congressional Districts</u>, (Lansing, Michigan: Employment
    Research Associates, 1979).

10. Minnesota, Wisconsin, Iowa, Illinois, Michigan, Indiana
    and Ohio.

11. Op. Cit., J.R. Anderson, pp. 2-3.

12. c.f. <u>Congressional Directory, 1979: 96th Congress, 1st
    Session</u>, (Washington, D.C.: U.S. Government Printing
    Office, 1979).

3. The Conversion of Military Economy: The USSR

The capability for carrying out conversion of industrial and allied resources from military to civilian economy has important bearing on the ability of a nation to participate in any reversal of the arms race.

In every nation that operates a large and durable military economy, the material and manpower resources devoted to this work have the inevitable effect of creating a special interest group that is tied to the continuation or expansion of military economy. That is owing to the unique occupational characteristics of managerial and technical occupations in the military economy, and to the power and privilege that is accorded to these occupations in the main military economies of the world.

During 1979-80 I completed a study for the United Nations on "Barriers to Conversion from Military to Civilian Industry--In Market, Planned and Developing Economies." Seven countries were studied: the USSR, US, UK, West Germany, Egypt, Israel and India. The following is a summary of findings of that investigation:

1. None of the governments examined enjoys an institutionalized capability for conversion in the form of planning staffs designed for or assigned to this purpose.

2. None of the governments has formulated plans that would require military production enterprises to develop civilian product alternatives.

3. In the market economies of western capitalism the internal economies of military enterprise are characterized by cost maximizing and subsidy maximizing. This differentiates them from the adjacent civilian economy and gives rise to basic occupational problems, in the event of

conversion, for the military-serving managers and engineers. The decision rules that produce success in military industry generate failure in the civilian sphere.

4. In the Soviet Union the enterprises of military economy are set off from those of the civilian economy by their high position in a priority system which governs access to every kind of supply for enterprise operation. The managers and engineers of Soviet military enterprise are thereby in positions of relative privilege and power vis-a-vis the managers and engineers of the civilian (lower priority) enterprise. The differences in privilege and power condition professional behavior.

5. The military economies of developing countries practice cost and subsidy maximizing, and also operate priority ranking systems for supply.

Importance of the Conversion Problem

Defining capability for economic conversion, and the barriers that must be overcome to achieve it, is an indispensable part of any serious effort to carry out a multinational reversal of the arms race. An end to the arms race means a change in the occupations of millions of men and women who are now specialists in weapons research and production.

The following are my 1979 estimates of the scale of the military industrial work forces in the countries of the UN inquiry:[1]

US (1974)	2,000,000
USSR	4,800,000
Federal Republic of Germany	325,000
Great Britain	600,000
Egypt	40,000
Israel	70,000
India	270,000

Military economy has become the sole livelihood for millions of men and women in industrialized and unindustrialized countries, notably for the many engineers, scientists and managers who are employed in disproportionately great numbers by the military economy. That job experience is highly specialized and differs everywhere from what is required by civilian industry. In the absence of alternatives, this specialization, locking large numbers of educated and well-paid people into the military economy, translates into a political commitment to the arms race and to its supporting technical and production activity.

For these reasons conversion capability is a vital measure of the willingness and ability of any society to participate in a reversal of the arms race.

The present paper focuses on the capabilities and limitations for economic conversion in the USSR. How able is the Soviet economy to redirect industrial resources from military to civilian service? Could a transition to civilian economy be carried out without major disruption; or does such conversion require deliberate advanced planning? Is industrial conversion purely a technical-engineering problem; or is it shaped by the basic qualities of the economic system as reflected in the characteristics of the managerial and technical occupation which govern Soviet manufacturing industry?

For this paper I have drawn upon the results of the inquiry conducted for the United Nations and have supplemented those data with materials from published literature as well as interviews with former Soviet scholars, technicians, and administrators who reported on their occupational experience in Soviet economy.

Data Limitations

The USSR has a central place in the realm of "planned economy." For that reason it is necessary to underscore, at the outset, four major limitations on the data concerning the USSR that were available for this inquiry.

First, remarkably little information has been published by the Soviet government on its military economy and on topics bearing on economic conversion in the USSR. Official data on the dimensions of the military economy—numbers of firms and factories, numbers of employees, budgets, wages and salaries, capital investments, research and development resources, etc.--are unavailable. Also, the available literature includes but two scant references to economic conversion in the USSR, both referring to experience following the Second World War.[2]

Second, Soviet authorities did not permit the present writer to interview any enterprise managers, or to visit any military industry enterprises.

A third limitation stems from compartmentalization of information on military economy matters among Soviet officials and institutions. Independently of intention, secrecy systems and "need to know" limitations on access to information segregate military economy and shield it from public scrutiny. Information on the number of enterprises

engaged in military production was not available at the
State Planning Committee (Gosplan).

A fourth limitation on data stemmed from evident lack
of attention to problems of economic conversion. Senior
policy and planning institutions in the USSR are frequently
uninformed concerning:
  a) lead time for planning industrial conversion;
  b) time needed for actual reconstruction of industrial
plants;
  c) differences in the occupational mix for civilian as
against military production;
  d) requirements for management (especially middle
management) retraining for economic conversion;
  e) requirements for engineering retraining;
  f) economic acceptability of civilian products manufactured to military design criteria.

Despite such limitations it was possible to make at
least a beginning in this inquiry toward defining problems of
conversion that are specific to Soviet economy. After all,
given armed forces of approximately 3.6 million, the scale of
the supporting industrial economy can be inferred--if only in
rough order of magnitude.

Thousands of enterprises and institutions are necessarily involved in military research, development and production.
These organizations must employ millions of industrial
workers, technicians, engineers, scientists, and managers.

Furthermore, the role of military economy vis-a-vis
civilian economy has undergone a historical development in
the USSR quite different from what occurred in the United
States and Western Europe. In the latter case the present
military economies were constructed alongside already fully
developed civilian economies. By contrast, in the USSR
after World War II industrial reconstruction and development
emphasized a heavy industry base and a collateral military
economy. This priority had an important bearing on the
subsequent development of civilian production and its relation to the military and allied heavy industry base.

Interviews in the USSR

Interviews were arranged through Soviet authorities
with a variety of knowledgeable people within the USSR,
including government officials and academic specialists.
Among the planning officials personally interviewed were a
senior official of the State Planning Committee of the USSR,
a senior official of the USSR State Committee for Science and
Technology (Council of Ministers), and a member of the

Central Committee of the Communist Party, USSR. Interviews
were also conducted with a number of specialists on industrial economics, including two senior officials and three
senior economists in research institutes of the USSR Academy
of Sciences, and a senior official of the Management Center,
Moscow State University; along with various senior industry
ministry officials, one at the ministry of machinery production and one at a major machinery research institute. A
labor economist and two Soviet journalists completed the
interview sample.

Data obtained from Soviet officials were supplemented
for this paper by interviews with former Soviet economists,
engineers, professors and administrators. These interviews
concentrated on the conditions of the managerial and engineering occupations in Soviet industry.

Supply and the Priority System

Supply is a central problem, quite possibly the central
problem, for both the managers of the national economy and
the managers of single enterprises in the Soviet system.
Problems of supply in the USSR are addressed within the
limits of a centralized priority system. A command economy
is operated in a context of shortages of goods so numerous
and pervasive that some Soviet authorities characterize
their economy as a deficit economy. Under such conditions,
there is no "marketing problem," no issue of finding pur-
chasers for all manner of goods.

The military economy of the USSR commands a large but
officially undesignated proportion of manufacturing resources
and manufacturing product. The proportion taken by the
military, however, is large enough so that priorities, as
between military and civilian uses, are discussed at the
highest levels of government.

Within the limits of priority allocation of capital and
allied resources to the military function, planning and
managing of the military economy are carried out separately
from that of civilian economy.

Cost Maximizing

An important, and interesting, problem of Soviet industrial micro-economy could not be properly resolved in this
inquiry. Are Soviet managers and engineers cost maximizers
(i.e., do they purposely produce at the highest cost they
can, subject to political acceptability constraints)? The
logic of the pervasive supply problem in Soviet industry
points in that direction. If supplies of virtually all

inputs are less than reliable, then managerial prudence would
dictate an effort to gain approval from higher authority for
plans that maximize supply allotments and minimize performance goals. That combination would best assure the manager
of success in the all-important matter of plan fulfillment.
While all Soviet industrial managers have an interest of
this sort, priority (military) industry managers should be
best situated to get the favorable conditions. In that
sense all Soviet managers are pressed to maximize cost relative to output, and this accounts for the several descrip-
tions by Soviet authorities of military industry managers:
military technology tends to overlook cost and give more
emphasis to performance; military engineers would make
civilian products so expensive no one could buy them; in
several cases when firms serving the military have turned to
civilian products they produced them at unacceptably high
cost. It seems possible that Soviet managers in military
industry are more successful cost maximizers than their
civilian counterparts.

A former Soviet industrial economist offers the following observation in this field:

> In the US military economy, managers act to
> maximize cost within the constraint of avail-
> able subsidy, but also to achieve higher
> output goals--that is, larger orders from
> the Department of Defense. This is owing
> to the fact that there have been few effective
> constraints on the availability of inputs for
> US military economy. By contrast, in the USSR,
> managers, even in military-serving enterprises,
> strive to get approval for low output and high
> cost. This is owing to the endemic problem
> on the supply side of virtually all factors
> of production in the Soviet system. And when
> costs are an approved part of the plan that
> is further insurance for plan-fulfillment--
> a vital result as it affects managerial and
> engineering bonus incomes and professional
> standing.

The foregoing is formulated as essentially theoretical
reasoning with a small data base. Regrettably, Soviet
authorities did not permit access to enterprise managers.

Planning for Conversion

Is there national planning for economic conversion?
Apparently not. Nor does any general policy require military
industry firms to prepare alternative product plans at the

enterprise level. The understanding of senior officials is that the development of such plans requires much labor, so they can't afford the outlay in the absence of a commitment to apply them.

At the same time senior Soviet officials are willing to say that here in Gosplan "we dream" about this process.   It would make life easier for the State Planning Committee because the military enterprises consume more valuable materials and research staff and more labor per unit--owing to the specifications for military products as against civilian ones--than are used even for good quality civilian production.   That being so, a shift to civilian economy would make it easier to "balance the economy."

The continuing response from Soviet economy managers to the problem of supply is a system of allocation according to priority ranking of enterprises.   The Handbook for Manufacturing Enterprise Directors sets up a formal salary ranking system for the top managers and other senior officials of Soviet Machine-building Industry firms.[3]   The ranking is based on a point weight system; and the main formal criteria are capital investment, number of employees and technical complexity of product.   The weights given to these factors assign enterprises to seven classes (Class 1 being the highest), with corresponding base salaries for the managing directors.   In addition to this formal ranking system, certain enterprises are ranked according to special considerations assigned to them by senior political officials.   Thus enterprises playing a key role in the priority goals of a Five-Year Plan are given top ranking.

A hierarchy corresponding to this one, or parallel to it, is apparently the primary operative system for the allocation of every sort of industrial input.   Suppliers of raw materials know that top-priority customers must be served with shipments of appropriate quantity and quality on the date specified and that it is the first obligation of the managers of the supplying enterprise to see to it that this is done.

Characteristically, high rank in the salary and supply priority system corresponds with ease of access to senior industrial ministry officials, ease of access to senior Communist Party officials and institutions, and all-around power and prestige for those enterprise managers.

The Manager's Job and Supply Priority

A senior official advises that solving the supply problems of an enterprise is a major managerial obligation.

Consider two aspects of supply: materials and engineers.
It is illuminating to see how a top priority management goes
about coping with these problems.

A senior official of a machinery producing ministry
receives a call for assistance from one of the ministry's
enterprises. The manager's production will be held up if
the supply of certain chemical raw materials is not immediately forthcoming. The manager in this case had been unable
on his own to arrange with the chemical industry for appropriate and timely supply, so he turned to the ministry. The
ministry official dealt with his opposite number in the
chemical industry ministry and was able, in short order, to
reach an agreement on the timing and quantity of shipment of
the needed materials. The ministry official explained:
sometimes we as a customer can help a supplier (chemical
enterprise) with the supply of equipment (industrial machinery) which we produce. This is the kind of leverage that
the top manager of a machinery producing industry has with
supplier firms that use his equipment. This relationship of
mutual leverage would of course not operate if one of the
parties were the manager in a low-priority enterprise--say,
a manufacturer of men's shirts.

The supply of materials can also be dealt with by
direct orders from top-level or party officials, who are
competent to order priority shipment of raw materials to
high priority firms. The general rule is apparently this:
the managers of high priority enterprises, including military serving enterprises, stand in line with everyone else;
but they are at the front of every supply line.

It is instructive to note also the mechanism by which
priority allocation operates in the supply of engineers to
enterprises of a high priority ministry. A ministry
official explained: how do we try to get the best engineers?
Our ministry's requests for engineers go to the State Plan-
ing Committee. The quota allotted to us is referred to a
technical institute that graduates engineers. Then of, say,
forty graduates from a Moscow institute we are allocated ten.
However, our access to engineers is further improved by the
fact that our ministry finances several laboratories at the
Moscow institute which work on contracts that we let.
Graduate students are employed on contracts in those laboratories. Hence we get to know the graduate students and can
decide which ones we prefer.

I asked this same manager: have you ever had or do you
have supply problems which you cannot solve? He said, no--
emphatically.

The problems and methods of operation for middle and low priority managers are rather different. These managers of medium to low ranked enterprises (with little or no access to top ministry officials) must, for example, resort to the "tolkach" for getting all sorts of supplies. The "tolkach" is an "expediter," often equipped with unaccountable funds and shrewd techniques for generating good will. By diverse methods, legal and extralegal, he must attempt to get deliveries of needed supplies to his firm, so that it can make an acceptable show of performing according to plan. That performance is, after all, the basis for staff salary bonuses and an important consideration for rating an enterprise manager.

Senior officials in the USSR acknowledge that the managers and engineers in military enterprise get the best materials and equipment. That is their privilege, and it gives them professional conditions which are unknown in the world of the lower priority managers.

Soviet enterprises typically employ a purchasing agent. But the wheeling and dealing and institutionalized illegalities that characterize the "tolkach" are concentrated in the lesser priority enterprises. A former tolkach reports that:

> The experience of the tolkach acting on behalf of the small enterprise is in sharp contrast to the observed experience of representatives of military industry firms. When a captain or a major representing a military industry firm goes to a supplier, the representative does not go to the sales, distribution or shipping department, but rather addresses the managing director or the chief engineer. In those cases, these officials typically turn to the visiting representative asking: what can we do for you? the relationship is altogether different from the characteristic one of dependence and powerlessness that surrounded the whole occupational experience of R.(a tolkach), as he represented his successive directors in relation to supply firms.

Managerial Power and Privilege

Managerial (and other employees) of high priority enterprises receive money incomes and incomes in-kind that are unique in Soviet society. Military serving enterprises

are assured to be typically concentrated in the top third
of the priority scale. I am advised that:

> The incomes that accrue to military
> industry managers include the follow-
> ing items: money salary and bonuses
> (monthly and annual); all manner of
> perquisites that attach to the office
> (cars, chauffeurs, houses, vacations,
> travel rights, etc.); prestige; social
> power (including and made visible by
> the ability to deal with others at the
> same level and the ability to reach
> political leaders directly--the number
> of telephones on a desk is a prime
> indicator of social power since each
> phone represents a separate, direct
> line network); economic managerial
> position in the town and region; the
> ability to have preferred access to
> all types of inputs (labor, machinery,
> raw materials, etc.) for the enterprise.

Money bonuses paid in addition to salary are monthly,
quarterly, semi-annual and annual. Monthly bonuses ranging
from 50 to as much as 100% of salary are awarded for plan
fulfillment, especially in an enterprise that has high
priority products. Quarterly bonuses are awarded for over-
fulfilling production and related plans and can amount to as
much as two months of salary. Annual bonuses can include
very large prizes. For example, a worker or engineer could
get two months additional salary payment on an annual basis.
The director typically receives the highest awards. Thus,
for fulfilling the technical and production plans, the
director can receive three to four months salary as the
annual bonus. In addition, special awards are given for
exceptional productivity and for technical innovation.

Non-salaried privileges include such things as better
supplies of food and consumer goods generally in the military serving towns than in other small towns. Housing is
characteristically much better supplied for the employees of
military industry enterprises. Thus the military enterprise
typically has a budget for constructing and operating housing for its staff so that workers can be supplied with an
apartment after about one year of employment. This is completely different from the experience of ordinary Soviet
citizens and employees in the civilian economy generally.

Soviet military industry managers are not only enterprise directors and party members, they are also, at times,

officers of the engineering corps (or engineering troops)
of the Red Army. Accordingly, such a manager may have the
title of Major of Technical Engineering in the army as well
as his rank as enterprise director. In that case he gets a
salary as a manager and also a salary for his military rank.
About 20% of managers are also military officers.[4]

Decision-power is a major aspect of priority differen-
tiated managerial posts. Thus a former Soviet industrial
economist observes that:

> As a manager of a military factory you are
> protected by the police, by the party, by
> the government, by the military and so
> forth, and a part of the control sector of
> the society. For a military manager to
> become the manager of a civilian firm is
> not just to lose privileges, but actually
> to lose power.

Some Technical Aspects of Industrial Conversion in the USSR

Soviet officials have affirmed that the civilian products of military enterprise tend to be of higher quality
than similar wares manufactured in wholly civilian enterprise. That is understandable, it reflects the higher
priority standing of military enterprises with respect to
all industrial inputs. Some Soviet planners affirm that,
this being the case, new civilian production from converted
military enterprise would most likely be competitive with
goods from existing civilian enterprise.

However, under conditions of variable access to industrial raw materials--according to the priority ranking of an
enterprise--a shift to civilian work may entail a decline in
product quality. The following was an exchange between the
author and a former engineer in a Soviet radio tube factory
that served the military:

> Suppose you were the chief engineer in
> that factory and you received an instruc-
> tion that 6 months hence you would be
> producing radio tubes for civilian use.
> What changes would you make in the design
> of your product?
>
> Mr. T. responsed: As soon as my main
> customer was civilian industry I would
> have less access to many critical materials

used in the manufacture of radio tubes.
The result would be that I would have
to make radio tubes for the civilian
market that had a lower quality, less
reliability, and more limited use life
as compared to the ones that I had made
for the military market.

Also, observers of Soviet military industry have noted
a repeated pattern of "mistakes" when such firms ventured
into civilian production. On some occasions, several such
enterprises in a given region have hit upon the same product
for their civilian entry, thus swamping the regional markets.

More significantly for the present inquiry, the quality
of civilian products turned out by military industrial firms
has at various times proven to be unacceptable. In several
cases the production cost of new civilian goods was so high
that it exceeded the conventional retail price of those
goods. This was true of certain radio and TV products.
High production costs occurred because some firms persisted
in applying to the civilian product the standards of design
and production they had grown accustomed to in the service
of the military.

Under Soviet conditions, differences in quality between
military and civilian industry have been due to more exact-
ing specifications for many military products. For example,
military organizations require communications devices of
high reliability, a quality indispensable for effective
command and control. The kind of unreliability that is
found in ordinary civilian telephone service, even in
Moscow, would not be acceptable.

Also, many conditions of potential military use impose
requirements that would have little or no civilian importance. For example, military equipment must endure rough
handling, frequent movement, and a range of temperature and
other climate conditions--all while maintaining a high level
of reliability.

None of this is to imply that the present inquiry has
discovered in Soviet military product design a parallel to
the "gold plating" of military products that is found in the
cost maximizing economies of the West ("gold plating" refers
to capabilities that are well in excess of reasonable requirements: use of expensive but functionally irrelevant
materials, excessive--and expensive--ornateness of design,
and attention to nonfunctional appearance). There is accu-
mulated evidence that Soviet military design, constrained by

the general condition of shortages, follows a more austere
tradition. The generalized condition of supply problems in
a deficit economy holds down the ceiling of subsidy below
which cost maximizing must function.

Conversion from military to civilian economy necessarily
involves changes of industrial equipment, but we have no
exact data on the characteristics of production equipment in
Soviet military industry. Even a sampling of such data was
not available for this study. We can only surmise that some,
perhaps a major, part of military industrial equipment is
"special purpose" in nature and would therefore have to be
scrapped or largely rebuilt for civilian product use.

The organization of civilian production in enterprises
serving the military is another technical feature bearing on
capability for conversion from military to civilian economy.
In an address before the Twenty-Fifth Congress of the Communist Party of the USSR in 1971, Leonid Brezhnev stated that
41 percent of the output of military industry consisted of
civilian products.[5] No further detail was given then or
since concerning any aspect of the stated intermix between
military and civilian output. (What is the definition of
the military serving entity? Is it the ministry, or a production unit with its own management and accounting statement?
Does the military serving industry include firms that manufacture steel or aluminum or tires or cement, part of whose
output supplies civilian industry? etc.) An intermix of
civilian and military output under the same top management of
an enterprise is a characteristic of military industry in
every country examined for the UN study.

From the standpoint of economic conversion it is crucial
to know how secondary civilian production is organized. What
proportion of that production is carried out under the same
roof as the military work? Does the civilian output utilize
production equipment similar to that of the military product
line, with differentiation only in the form of special tool-
ing, so that the civilian work is convertible in relatively
few days to higher military product capacity? Similarly,
could the military production line be converted to civilian
work? (This depends on the degree to which specialized as
against general purpose production equipment is used in both
the military and the civilian work.) Or is the civilian
production carried out in a division of the enterprise that
is organizationally and spatially separate from the military
work, with a separate management, and so on? Several
observers have reported that both types of organizations are
to be found in Soviet military-civilian enterprise, but the
data are fragmentary.

It may be significant that some Soviet planners underscore the desirability of the diversification pattern
practiced in US industrial firms. This ordinarily involves
financial diversification, accompanied by separate organization and operation of civilian production. In this case
the financial assets of the firm are "diversified," but, as
said earlier, that does not necessarily bear on the problem
of converting production resources from military to civilian
work.

A Soviet management consultant reports that there are
two types of military-civilian enterprise, one in which
military and civilian products are technically the same, as
in the case of aluminum for aircraft and for cooking
utensils, and one in which civilian products are assigned
to military enterprise independently of technical connection.
For example, in a recent year, owing to weather conditions
and equipment shortages, there was an urgent need for hay-
drying machines; the Kama River Truck Factory was assigned
this special machinery order. (Note that this could have
been readily accommodated by the general purpose equipment
that surely forms part of the machinery stock of any very
large factory of this class.)

According to this management consultant, the latter
situation is more typical of the problem of converting from
military to civilian work, because the former is easy.

Appropriate time allowances for blueprinting and imple-
menting major industrial changes are an important technical
aspect of economic conversion planning and capability.
Actual "lead times" for these purposes are an important
aspect of industrial operations planning in any economy, but
tend to be less well understood among Soviet policy officials and macroeconomic planners.

Managers of Soviet machinery producing industries, on
the other hand, appear to be well-informed about lead time
requirements and problems in a product conversion situation.
Consider the possibility of converting from, say, steam
turbine generators to hydro-turbine generators. What is
needed is an advance plan. Its implementation would require
the help of the ministry, since the ministry has decision
power over capital investment and equipment. Most important,
it would be necessary to change the production plan of the
enterprise and to make allowance for transition time and to
provide for "working capital" for the changeover.

According to industry officials, the time for making a
major conversion could be illustrated by the problem of

changing the products of an enterprise from AC to DC motors.
For this changeover (to a closely related product) a planning
time of about six months would be required. Implementation
of the blueprint for new products takes up to one and a half
years for the completed factory reconstruction, with partial
production starting before the end of the period. This reconstruction period includes time for retraining engineers
and managers and production workers.

While the above considerations are evidently understood
among Soviet industrial managers -- necessarily so -- the
role of lead time is apparently not uniformly appreciated
among Soviet economists and policy officials. This creates
an important disconnection between policy makers and the industrial production realities that are subject to their decision. This defines a limitation of the capability of the
Soviet economy for conversion planning and implementation.

Conversion of Management Occupations

The managers of Soviet military enterprise have a special
relation to the military economy. Their priority position
gives them special power and privilege compared to the managers of civilian enterprise. The problems of supply of every
sort of industrial input -- which dominate the managerial
occupations of the Soviet Union -- are handled with relative
ease by the military industry managers.

Among students of Soviet industrial management it is apparently well understood that in military enterprise the
managers pay more attention to technical than to supply problems. The latter can be solved with the help of the supporting system of ministry officials, party chiefs, supplier
management and top government officials -- all of whom are
committed to seeing that the supply requirements of military
industry are given first priority. One result of this pre-
ferential treatment is that there is, according to a senior
management consultant, a "real difference between civil and
military enterprise, in that the military managers are more
engineering oriented, while the civilian managers are more
businessmen."

Some theorists in Soviet society judge that such considerations have no real importance for economic conversion and
that military industrial managers will simply have to obey
the order of higher authority to change the nature of goods
produced. It is also noted that, despite their privileges,
military industry managers sometimes envy their civilian
counterparts; the military managers are relatively unknown to
the general public, owing to the strict security that sur-

rounds them and their work. By way of illustration there is
the case of two important academicians (unnamed), one known
to the whole country and one who cannot talk about his work
even to his own family. It is argued that this anonymity is
an important negative factor in the relative status of military and civilian managers.

However, as questions about the convertibility of military industry managers to civilian occupations were discussed with people who are close to or part of industrial management operating networks, another view of the matter emerged.
Consider the prototypic case of a military enterprise managing director who is informed by his ministry that he has been
assigned to take charge, six months hence, of establishing
and then operating a new and large industrial enterprise to
manufacture refrigerators. Apart from every other consideration, the manager in question knows that he is being asked to
move from a high priority to a middle priority industrial
enterprise. This causes immediate concern about the apparent
demotion: the prospective loss of power and privilege. Some
Soviet students of industrial management conclude that the
military industry managers know that, if conversion comes,
their privilege will be demolished.

One set of responses would utilize positive and negative
incentives to accept conversion. A variety of possibilities
exist. For one, salaries could be increased as an economic
incentive. They might also be simply ordered to transfer or
lose their jobs in the ministry (not dissimilar to the pattern sometimes employed by multinational corporations in
making unpleasant assignments). Managers, especially middle
managers would also have to be retrained for administrative
routines in civilian firms that are necessarily different
from their specialized experience within military industry
and in relation to the Soviet Ministry of Defense.

Another positive incentive would involve ending the anonymity of the ex-military industry manager, drawing public
attention to him/her and his/her achievements. Or, one might
try to apply social pressure by an appeal to patriotism.

Such steps, while possibly effective in moving many individual managers, are not necessarily a sufficient response
to a situation where the prospect of economic conversion
would affect large numbers of industrial managers at the
same time. In that case another factor enters the scene:
the possibility of group pressure by military industry managers to protect their privilege, their power.

In an interview with a top manager of a machinery produc-

ing ministry I asked about the existence of contingency conversion plans for a shift from present to alternative products. He responded: "What do you mean by conversion? You
surely wouldn't expect us to convert to the manufacture of
sausages!" (hearty laughter.)

In fact **sausages**, meaning processed food, or simple
household goods, or the equipment for making them well and
cheaply, may be important parts of what the USSR needs in
considerable quantity to raise both the level of living and
the level of productivity. But industrial production of
these **sausages** has been associated with lesser privileges and
power. Accordingly, the top manager's amused comment reflects where he now stands in the power structure, and states
the sort of thing he would **not** wish to do in the interest of
maintaining or enhancing his managerial position and political stature.

That is a core issue of management economic conversion
that must be addressed as part of planning for conversion in
the USSR.

Conversion of Engineering Occupations

Data concerning the number of Soviet engineers and scientists working in military as against civilian enterprise
and institutions are not available. However, it is safe to
assume that the group is very large. This is indicated by
the characteristics of modern weaponry, and by the structure
of employment in military industry of other countries, where
engineers often outnumber production workers.

A senior administrator of a major industrial research
institution in Moscow says that:

> from my contacts with manufacturing and other
> enterprises, I believe that all present plants
> and engineering groups could readily add ten
> percent to their staffs. Seven or eight years
> ago we could have had a problem because of a
> lack of jobs for scientific workers and engin-
> eers. Now we have problems that need increasing
> staff. The problems of a ten percent increase
> in staff are soluble within about 1.5 years,
> needed for the requisite training time. This
> would include not only new facilities for working
> (as in our Institute), but also housing for the
> staff.

Occupational conversion of engineers from military to

civilian serving enterprises must take into account a change
in qualifications. In Soviet experience military technology
tends to overlook cost and to emphasize performance.

A senior research administrator affirms that Soviet
engineers, qualified in military industry, must be retrained
to design for performances that are appropriate to civilian
functions, while achieving such standards at acceptable cost.
At the same time, they must be encouraged to transfer appropriate technologies developed in the military sphere to civilian tasks -- for example, the design and use of computers.

Informed judgment in the Soviet Union is that scientists
require about a year of retraining and adaptation to fit them
for transfer from military to civilian serving institutions.
For engineers the task is seen as somewhat more difficult.
One estimate is that it is infeasible to transfer engineers
directly from military to civilian work without declassify-
ing aspects of military technology for application to civilian uses.

At the same time, said one engineer-administrator: I
would not put military engineers on (heavy machinery) apparatus. They would make products so expensive that no one would
buy them. I would put them on components.

What retraining time is needed for engineers and scientists? What should be the context of such retraining, and
who will pay for it? Repeated experience in the Soviet Union
indicates that a retraining period of one to two years is a
reasonable requirement for carrying out the necessary specialized training (and unlearning).

Retraining of engineers can be accomplished in various
ways. One could use existing technical schools at the larger
enterprises. The ministry in each case allocates funds to
prepare the work force, as, for example, for a new enterprise, which may require the retraining of as many as two
thousand people. On occasion, several neighboring enterprises might join to establish a school for this purpose.

A second possible method is to send engineers and skilled workers for on-the-job training in an enterprise that is
already producing the new product. The appropriateness of
this form of training would depend on the complexity of the
product.

A third form of technical training would borrow engineers and workers from other enterprises and send them to the
enterprises being reconstructed to serve as instructors for

on-the-job training. In such cases, the people sent to do
the training would be given some priorities in housing and
income increases, especially the young and unusually capable
engineers and workers, who would have difficulty in getting
promotions and privileges within the framework of already
established firms.

Soviet management consultants indicate that there are
three essential patterns or styles of operation for making
use of engineers made excess by a turn away from military
engineering. Individuals might be given free choice to join
civilian industries of diverse sorts; engineering jobs inside
the military industry might be changed; or a deliberate program of re-education might be undertaken. The latter could
be accomplished by a system of advanced studies for the engineers and related occupations. Under the present Soviet law
an ex-employer is responsible for such retraining. One
opinion is that the government should pay for it; however,
there is no present law and budgeting provision for government to undertake this retraining on a large scale.

These views of knowledgeable Soviet managers and analysts
fall short of meeting the problems that would develop if a
large number of engineers and scientists had to be moved from
military to civilian serving enterprises and institutions.
In that case there would be problems not only of occupational
retraining, but also of providing adequate housing and community facilities. For example, the conversion of aerospace
industry factories to rail vehicle production would free the
majority of engineers involved for other work, but their relocation in thousands would require substantial advance planning and preparation.

None of this is to say that under Soviet conditions
there may not be alternatives to major relocations of engineers and related occupations. After all, no law of nature
precludes bringing the work -- the industrial and allied
facilities -- to where the people are, instead of staging
occupational migration to the facilities. However, these and
other alternatives were not brought up by Soviet officials in
various interviews. It is entirely possible that they failed
to do so because the occupational problems occasioned by conversion from military to civilian economy have not yet been
thought through in the USSR.

Summary of Findings

The economy of the Soviet Union has potential planning
capability for economic conversion. There is no evidence,
however, of current preparations to cope with the specific

economic, technological and organizational problems associated with conversion from military to civilian economy. This
applies to both aggregate and local enterprise planning.

In the USSR planning for occupational and organizational
conversion, at both industry and enterprise levels, must take
into account the sustained and pervasive operation of the
priority economic targeting system, which ranks enterprises
with special reference to supply priorities of every kind.
Priority ranking has a substantial effect on the power, privilege and methods of operation of all managers and engineers.

Apart from every substantive economic and industrial
consideration discussed here, there is a structural-institu-
tional matter that constrains Soviet potential for economic
conversion. At this writing the Soviet Union has yet to designate a group of professionals as being responsible for defining and addressing the industrial conversion problems of
their own country. That means: there is no literature on
conversion in the USSR; no formulation of alternatives, production plans, no debate on policy alternatives and limited
knowledge of these topics even among otherwise serious and
highly qualified people.

Implications of Findings

With respect to economic conversion, the similarities
among the countries examined far outweigh the differences.
Whatever the national differences of size, wealth, culture,
geography, history, power, social and economic structure, the
governing establishment of the USSR (as in the US, UK, West
Germany, Egypt, India and Israel) has no contingency plans
for economic conversion of the military economy. Diverse
ideological rationalizations are advanced in these countries
to justify a common decision: neither aggregate nor enterprise level contingency planning should be done for economic
conversation. The decision not to do alternative use planning is paralleled, in each government, by the absence of
assigned professional responsibility for developing workable
blueprints for reversing the arms race.

Within each of these nations the military-industrial
economy controls the largest block of industrial production
resources under one management. These industrial systems
enjoy subsidies that are generous beyond the hopes of the
rest of society. Their internal operations are typically
free from pressures for minimizing cost or for greater productivity.

For the state managerial establishment of each nation,

the military-industrial network is the basis for dominion
over scientists, engineers, managers and production workers.
The capital intensity typical of military industry marks its
rulers as the top economic decision makers of each society.
The military/economic position leads readily to political
power through the particular institutional channels of each
nation.

Under best possible conditions, a sustained operation of
large military economies cannibalizes the civilian host economies. The civilian end products of this process vary with
economic structure: in the U.S. depressed productivity
growth, inflation and unemployment; in the USSR depressed
productivity growth, inflation and severe shortages.

Under worst possible conditions, large military economies
in the service of the unwinnable nuclear arms race hasten
World War III and the termination of the human community.

The hawkish majorities of the Soviet Politburo and the
American government have not permitted the development of
government-based economic conversion capability. Nevertheless, there is an important difference between the Soviet-
type society and others, notably the U.S., Canada, England,
Sweden, Norway, Denmark, (West) Germany, France, Italy. In
these countries scholars at universities, and independent
political and activist groups of all sorts, have been addressing the economic conversion problem. By exercising the right
of independent organization -- whose importance can hardly be
overstated -- they have developed a coherent and growing body
of knowledge on the characteristics and consequences of war
economies, and on the requirements for workable conversion
from military to civilian economy. A U.S. peace organization,
SANE, of which I have the honor to be co-Chairman, treats
conversion as a program priority, and publishes a periodical
titled Conversion Planner. A growing array of regional and
local conversion project groups in key military industry
areas are projecting the conversion idea and training people
in these strategies. A widening circle of trade unionists is
viewing economic conversion as a vital part of restoring the
industrial economic competence in the U.S. and other western
countries. (See Chapter Eight.) The conversion planning
initiative of the unions at Lucas (Aerospace Division) in
England is of historic importance (see Chapter Seven).

Nevertheless, all that does not take away from the fact
that during the great armaments build-up that has followed
World War II, the disposition of military economy, hence the
conversion problem, has been the item omitted from the agenda
of every meeting among states to consider the arms race in

any respect. Therefore even a beginning of conversion capability within the nation-states will be a start toward reversing the arms race among the states.

That is why it is important to identify the barriers to economic conversion and to find ways to surmount them everywhere.

References

1. The US datum (1974) is from the US government's response to UN queries, in UN, General Assembly, Economic and Social Consequences of the Armament Race and its Extremely Harmful Effects on World Peace and Security, 12 September 1977, p. 140. The USSR estimate was prepared as follows: 3.6 million in armed forces, from Sivard, R.L., World Military and Social Expenditures, 1979, p. 25; assuming (as in the US) a 1:1 relation between personnel in armed forces and supporting civilian industry, adjusted for USSR productivity in military industry assumed 75% of US, then USSR military industry estimated as using 4.8 million employees. The West German figure is a best estimate from informed persons. The Great Britain estimate is derived from Sense About Defense: The Report of the Labour Party Defense Study Group (Quartet Books, 1977), p. 16. Egypt and Israel data are from the respective ministries of defense. The India datum is from the Government of India, Ministry of Defense, Report, 1978-79, New Delhi, 1979.

2. Leitenberg, Milton, USSR Military Expenditure and Defense Industry Conversion: An Introduction and Guide to Sources (Center for the Study of Armament and Disarmament, California State University Los Angeles, Los Angeles, California 90032, 1980).

3. Egiazaryan, G.A. and A.D. Sheremet, eds., Handbook for Manufacturing Enterprise Directors, Vol. 11 (Moscow: Economics Publishing House, 1977), p. 131.

4. c.f. Mathews, M., Privilege in the Soviet Union--A Study of Elite Life Styles Under Communism (London: Allen and Unwin, 1978); Andrle, V., Managerial Power in the Soviet Union (Lexington, Massachusetts: Lexington Books, 1976).

5. In the U.S. (1978) 60 percent of the output of the hundred largest Department of Defense contracting firms was civilian. That reflects the product diversification of the larger U.S. industrial conglomerates.

4. The Social and Economic Consequences of the Military Influence on the Development of Industrial Technologies

It is well known that the military has played and still plays an important role in stimulating technological development, especially in wartime. Everyone has heard at least some of the war stories about radar, nuclear energy, electronics, computers, fighter aircraft, and control and communications systems. All of these technologies, and the list is endless, were created to serve purposes peculiar to the military: proximity fuses for bombs, submarine and aircraft detection, combat communications, rocketry and missile warfare, gunfire control, ballistics calculations, command and control defense networks, high speed, versatile flight, atomic and nuclear weapons. Yet, despite these original objectives, it is a common conception that such military-born technologies as these "spill over," as the story goes, into civilian use, where they are then adapted for a host of other, more benign and even beneficial, purposes. This is the conventional account of the role of the military in technological development. Essentially, this military role is characterized in two ways. First, it is what economists would call "exogenous" as far as the civilian economy is concerned; military-born technologies enter the economy from "outside," so to speak, in a random, unsystemic way. (Of course, this is the way economists view all technological development; for them, military technologies merely combine two exogeneities, the military, or government, and technology.) Second, the military influence on the development of the technologies is only temporary and "restricted" to the actual military uses of the technologies, for weaponry and the like. That is, the military influence does not permanently mark the technologies nor does that military influence in any way spill over along with the technologies when they undergo transfer from the military to the civilian arenas.

I would like to suggest that this conventional view of the role of the military in technological development is problematic on both counts. First, the military role has not been as exogenous, as external as it appears to be when viewed through the lens of the neoclassical economist. Rather, it has been central to industrial development in the U.S. since the dawn of the industrial revolution. Lewis Mumford, among others, has been arguing this for some time, but it has been terribly difficult for us to shake the economists' habit as well as the peculiarly American blindness to the effects of the presence of the military. Second, the influence of the military on the technologies is not temporary, something removed when the technologies enter the civilian economy. The influence spills over in the specific shape of the technologies themselves and in the ways they are put together and used, with far-reaching economic and social consequences that have barely been examined.

The preceding chapters have described some of the consequences of the military role in the economy. They have discussed the vast military pre-emption material, technical and labor resources that might be used to meet human needs were they not diverted toward nonproductive, wasteful and dangerous military objectives. They have pointed out the corrupting influences of cost maximizing military procurement and contracting practices that have given rise to generations of managers incapable of truly independent, innovative, efficient or economical production, and to legions of technical personnel who are incompetent to produce for a competitive market (or otherwise meet such non-military specifications as cheapness, simplicity, accessibility and the like). But there are still other ways, more subtle perhaps, in which the military shapes technological and industrial development, with consequences that are no less profound.

In 1965, the U.S. Air Force produced a film to promote the use of numerical control manufacturing methods in the military-oriented aerospace industry.[1] The new technology had been developed over the previous decade and half under Air Force aegis. The film well reflects the scope of the military penetration into private industry, ranging from aircraft manufacture to machine tools, electronic controls and communications, and computers (Republic Aviation, Lockheed, Hughes, Giddings and Lewis, Pratt and Whitney, Sundstrand, Kearney and Trecker, Raytheon, IBM: all are in the film). The film also illustrates what I will refer to as the dominant characteristics of the military approach to industrial development, characteristics which, taken together, constitute a system of thinking that informs, embraces and transcends the particular technical developments themselves. For purposes of simplicity, I have reduced these to three basic

preoccupations: "performance," "command," and so-called
"modern methods."

By "performance" is meant the emphasis placed upon meeting military objectives, and what follows necessarily from
it. These objectives include, for example, combat readiness,
tactical superiority, and strategic responsiveness and control, and these objectives demand such things as -- in the
case of the Air Force -- fast, versatile, and powerful aircraft; keeping up with the arms race for ever-more sophisticated weaponry; and worldwide communications and control.
These secondary objectives require another set of manufacturing specifications: the capability to manufacture highly complex yet reliable parts for high speed aircraft and missiles
(airfoils, variable thickness skins, integrally stiffened
wing sections, etc.); short lead-time and turn-around time
to accommodate rapid design changes; and, perhaps most important, interchangeability, reproducibility, and compatibility
vital to an integrated system, what Professor Merritt Roe
Smith has aptly called "the uniformity principle."[2]

These military performance objectives are justified in
the name of national survival, and so too are the product
specifications and manufacturing criteria that follow from
them. Note that cost has not yet been mentioned. Certainly,
it is an important consideration, but only a secondary one,
crucial only insofar as it is "consistent with reliability
and reproducibility," to quote the film. There is no direct
concern whatsoever for meeting market demands or social or
human needs. (2) Command: Lucas Aerospace engineer Michael
Cooley has referred to management as "a bad habit inherited
from the church and the military." I do not know about the
church's influence upon management but the military's is
certainly clear. The military term for management is "command," a rather straightforward notion which means the superior gives the orders and the subordinate executes them, with
no if's, and's, or but's. It is the ideal of all managers
everywhere. In the private sector it follows, with more or
less legitimacy, from the pursuit of profit, control, and the
will to power. In the military, it follows from the need to
meet performance objectives. Uniformity in manufacture, for
example, presupposes command, direct and uncompromised. This
is well illustrated by the film. First, the film has been
made for top management, not the workforce who will actually
be doing the work. The film's theme -- the proposed and
promised aim of modern manufacturing is "to shorten the chain
of command" and to "greatly reduce the opportunities for a
breakdown in communication." That means that there will be
less human intervention between order and execution and those
who remain will perform "reliably," according to "fixed"
instructions which are "not subject to human error or

emotion." Thus, there will be no reliance upon the autonomy, skill, initiative, creativity of people who stand between the commander and the machinery. The dream, the supreme management fantasy, is well depicted at the beginning of the film when the top manager voices his commands into the microphone: "orders to the plant." "Humans do what they do best," create, so long as by "humans" we mean top management; on the other hand, "machines do what they do best," the automatic following of orders, down to the last detail. And this brings us to the last characteristic military preoccupation, "modern methods." Modern manufacturing means a fetish for machinery, which won't talk back, a preoccupation with capital intensive production. Modern means NC production machinery, computers, assembly robots, plotters and drafting machines, inspection, testing equipment, transfer machines, machines for automatic welding, forming, pipe-bending, assembly robots, and the like. These are the "elements of our plan of the future." People, except for top management and designers, disappear from view almost entirely. Indeed, "modern" specifically means machines, to be contrasted with "conventional" meaning people. But conventional also means "backward" or "primitive" and this gives force to the modernizing drive. This is illustrated, in a racist if otherwise unintentionally humorous way, by scenes of half-clad natives making iron by hand and even operating a lathe in a thatched hut. The message is clear: conventional means reliance upon people and people mean error, emotion, primitiveness. The ideal of the military, and of the managers who have inherited the military habit, is the automatic factory ("factory on/factory off"). In the meantime, the military system of manufacture means a highly regimented system of people, temporary place-holders for the robots of the future, who are paced and disciplined by the machinery which has come under direct management command.

Performance, command, modern methods. These then are the dominant characteristics of the military approach to industry, justified in the name of national security and enforced throughout industry by the system of military procurement contracts. The DOD "expects defense contractors to maintain a modern base in their facilities," the film concludes. Within the military framework, all of this makes perfect sense; it is logical, supremely rational. But it becomes irrational in other contexts, as the military approach spills over, permeates, and diffuses throughout the economy, carried in the form of performance requirements, habits of command, and machine designs. Because in other contexts the objectives are different. The focus is on meeting social and human needs through the production of cheap goods and services; meeting the demands of a competitive market; fostering the kinds of things all Americans profess to value: self-reliance, democracy, life, liberty, and the pursuit of happiness. The rationality of the military is not always compatible with these objectives. More important, it is often destructive of these objectives. It increases costs while using up valuable resources. It devalues human judgment, skill, autonomy, self-reliance, initiative, and creativity. It leads to the actual depletion and atrophy of the store of inherited human skills. In its fetish for capital intensive production, it contributes to the dislocation and displacement of untold numbers of workers and possibly to massive structural unemployment. It fosters, in its emphasis upon command, what Mumford has called an "authoritarian" rather than a "democratic" technics, and thus, in the name of order, creates social instability and mounting industrial tensions. In its insistence upon uniformity and system integration, it fosters ever increasing complexity and, it correlates greater flexibility and unreliability. And finally, it places human beings, the subjects of society, of history, of production, in a subordinate role to military objectives, to the commands that flow from those objectives, and to the machinery that automatically executes those commands. Nothing could be more irrational, or more frightening.

It might appear to some, by this time, that I am simply arguing against progress, against technology, against mechanization and automation per se. This is not true. Indeed, quite the contrary, I applaud new ways of doing things as much as the next person. But I try to discipline myself, temper my fascination and enthusiasm, by looking hard at the proposed uses of the technologies and the likely consequences, the human and social costs, the potential for greater or less happiness. This is what I understand to be rationality. Progress for what? What kind of progress? Progress for whom?

With these questions in mind, I would like to examine, more closely and concretely, three examples of the military influence on industrial and technological development. So as not to show favoritism or bias, I have selected one illustration from each service, the Army, the Navy, and the Air Force. My apologies to the Marines. Each example describes a major technological change in which the military played a central role: interchangeable parts manufacture, containerization, and numerical control. Without question, these were major technical accomplishments, with far-reaching if ambiguous consequences for the civilian economy. In military terms, as well as in technical terms, these were magnificent departures from tradition, bold steps forward for progress. They also well reflect the dominant military characteristics that I have enumerated: performance, command, and modern methods. And they also illustrate that there have been costs unaccounted for, serious questions, begged by the ideology of progress, which have yet to be confronted fully by any of us.

Army: Interchangeable Parts

In the first half of the 19th century, the Ordnance
Department which ran the country's arsenals and armories
evolved an ideology of uniformity. The performance objective
underlying this ideology was to insure the ready field repair
of firearms through the supply of interchangeable spare parts.
The impulse behind all this stemmed from the difficulties en-
countered in the War of 1812. (Incidentally, the only reason
the U.S. emerged victorious in that conflict was because the
enemy, Great Britain, was embattled also on two other fronts:
Napoleon on one, the Luddites on another. It has been estimated that England had as many troops in the Midlands fighting the displaced hand-loom weavers as in America fighting the
U.S.) The problems faced in that war prompted the Ordnance
Department to search for better ways. Under the direction of
men like Decius Wadsworth, George Bomford, George Talcott and
others, the Army began earnestly to promote the pioneering
methods of inventors like John Hall and Simeon North, to try
to establish uniformity in the manufacture of firearms at both
Springfield and Harper's Ferry arsenals and at the plants of
private contractors. This performance criterion became something of an obsession. As one self-described "soldier-tech-
nologist," Major Alfred Mordecai, explained in 1861, "my ability
consists in a knowledge and love of order and system and in
the habit of patient labor in perfecting and arranging de-
tails." And the performance criteria of uniformity neces-
sitated the establishment of command over all productive operations, heretofore relatively autonomous. This was effected
by the establishment of an ongoing bureaucracy, in Smith's
words, for the "specific regulation of the total production
process from the initial distribution of stock to the final
accounting of costs." The whole system came to be viewed as
a "complex machine." And, at the heart of the system were
the modern methods of manufacture, the physical embodiment of
"fixed orders": the hardened steel gauges, the patterns, the
special machines and fixtures, which replaced human craft,
skill in producing, testing and evaluating parts, and thereby
eliminated human error and insured uniformity.

The effective use of these new methods required tighter
management control and supervision, the elimination not only
of traditional skills but also of traditional work patterns
and routines grounded in the autonomy of the craftsman. Uniformity of parts was followed soon by uniformity in housing,
in working hours, in shop discipline, presaging the scientific management of the next century (another product of the
arsenals). The uniformity system was imposed on contractors
by the military contract system; Bomford "apprised private
manufacturers that the issuance of future arms contracts

would depend on their performance, especially the degree to
which they updated their operations."

   As is well known, the uniformity system developed in the
arsenals became the basis of the so-called American system of
manufactures, characterized by special machinery, precise
gauges and interchangeability of parts. Men left the arms
business to set up the machine tool industry and went on from
there to carry the principle of uniformity into the manufacture of railroad equipment, sewing machines, pocket watches,
typewriters, agricultural implements, bicycles, and so on.
The rest, as they say, is history, the history of progress.

   But there was another side to this story, which we have
not heard much about. First, not everyone was enthusiastic
about the uniformity system, and that does not only mean the
workers who had to buckle under to tighter discipline. "As
impressive as they were," Smith reminds us, "these accomplishments tended to obscure fundamental ambiguities and tensions associated with the introduction of the uniformity
system. Conflicting opinions existed over the need for
mechanization as well as the importance of uniformity."
Many people were skeptical, such as those Harper's Ferry
workers and managers who for forty years successfully re-
sisted the introduction of the full system. Smith reports
also that "similar feelings existed among some contractors,
although they were less willing to oppose the uniformity
policy for fear of losing their contracts." It is interesting to note that, without the new system, Harper's Ferry
continued for some thirty years to match the output of
Springfield, where the system was first installed.

   The benefits of the system, clear to the military, were
not so clear to many manufacturers, given the high cost, un-
certainties, and inescapable industrial conflict it engendered. Moreover, the system proved a disaster for those who
lost their jobs, were subjected to much tighter discipline,
and suffered the deskilling and degradation that always
accompanies "modern methods." Not surprisingly, class conflict "seethed beneath the glowing veneer of industrial
achievement." To those who planned and orchestrated the uniformity system" Smith concludes "all the changes seemed fully
compatible with their ideas of rational design [but] to those
who worked under the system, the new regimen represented a
frontal assault on valued rights and privileges."

Navy: Containerization[4]

   In July, 1952, at the initiative of the military (the
Chief of Naval Research, and representatives from the Army

and Marines), the National Research Council (NRC) Committee
on Amphibious Operations held a joint government-industry
conference on marine cargo handling and transport. The <u>per-</u>
formance objective of the military was the improvement of
cargo transport efficiency and the elimination of potential
dock tie-ups, so as to improve U.S. undersea warfare capability and guarantee logistical support for military operations.
The military had for some time been doing research in the
area while the industry had done nothing, and the military,
for its purposes, sought to promote joint government-industry
research to improve maritime efficiency. A year later the
S.S. Warrior study was conducted by the NRC, to determine precisely what the inefficiencies were in cargo handling. A few
years after that the NRC conducted the San Francisco Port
Study under the direction of Admiral E. G. Fullingwider, to
document the inefficiencies of longshoring. Shortly thereafter, in 1960, the famous "Mechanization and Modernization
Plan" was agreed upon by the Pacific Maritime Association and
the ILWU, West Coast Longshoremen's union. Essentially, here
modernization meant the substitution of standardized containers for loose cargo, the replacement by the container ships
(to accommodate them) of conventional freighters, and the
substitution of large docks and cranes for finger piers and
longshoremen. In short, Plan meant the elimination of traditional longshoring. Pushed by the military, the container
revolution was "greatly accelerated" by the demands of the
Vietnam War. More recently, the second container revolution
has begun, with the computerization of crane-loading operations.

   The conventional system of longshoring was marked by the
gang system, essential cooperative teamwork, and a decentral-
ization of initiative, innovation and skill. Since each ship
was different in its construction and each load of cargo was
unique to the job, there was an endless variety of tasks and
inviolable autonomy for the gang as it tried to solve unique
problems. The work itself was governed by specific work
rules which specified manning, load limits, and safety standards. The hiring hall was an egalitarian institution which
guaranteed a fair distribution of work among union members,
with its principle of low man out. Both the work rules and
the hiring hall were won by the union through decades of
bitter struggle, highlighted by the 1934 strike. Beyond the
work itself, but essential to the longshore culture was ongoing conversation, comradery between partners and lively and
informal work groups and a vital dock community. The container revolution changed all this. Cargo packaged in containers
(and loaded and unloaded away from the dock) was now standardized as were the ships designed to carry them and thus
the dockwork now dominated by the large cranes became routin-
ized and subject to closer control and discipline. On the

large container docks the workforce was atomized. The new
methods broke up the gangs and informal work groups, put an
end to close contact, conversation and comradeship and dec-
imated the dock community. Work rules were surrendered by
the union and the principle of institutionalized justice in
the hiring hall was violated by the introduction of "steady
men," crane operators, whose presence was justified in the
name of expensive and sophisticated equipment and the skills
they supposedly demanded (this remains a controversial issue).
The chain of command was thus shortened, with the displacement of the majority of longshoremen and the close and re-
lentless supervision of equipment operators. "Throughout
the shift," crane operators "are simply told by radio or
computer print-out where to pick up or place their next container. There is no occasion for initiative or innovation
on their part nor is there any on-going operational need for
their employers to in any way consult with them."[5]

Again, performance, command, modern methods. Backed by
the military, employers argued "you can't hold back progress.
You just can't fight the machine," and the union buckled under, holding on to privileges for the few at the expense of
the many. But for the longshoremen as a whole, their union,
and their communities, as well as for their hard won dignity,
and workplace principles of autonomy and equality, this progress was a disaster. Lincoln Fairley, Research Director of
the ILWU 1946-67 originally a strong supporter of the Mechanization and Modernization Plan, has changed his mind. "As
experience under the Plan developed," he writes, "I began to
share with many of the longshoremen doubts about how it was
working out from the standpoint of the men. Not only did the
gains to the employers far outstrip the gains to the union
and its members but, at least in this case, the union was
weakened and the employers regained much of the ground they
had lost in the 1930's. The presumed social and economic
benefits deriving from a modernized and more efficient
industry are no adequate offset." Even Harry Bridges, the
ILWU President who made the historic deal, has had second
thoughts. As Fairley reports "it is known that Mr. Bridges
believes the Plan to have been a mistake."

Air Force: Numerical Control[6]

Numerical control (NC) was completely underwritten by the
U.S. Air Force, including research and development, software
development, actual purchase of machinery for contractors,
and training of programmers and operators. Total cost was
over $60 million. As already indicated the performance ob-
jectives were high speed aircraft and missiles, requiring
complex machining capability and uniformity. The NC revolution, as it came to be called, was fueled by the Korean War

and the Cold War of the 1950's and 60's. The <u>command</u> impera-
tive entailed direct control of production operations not
only with a single machine or within a single plant but
worldwide, via data links. The vision of the architects of
the NC revolution involved much more than the automatic machining of complex parts. It meant the elimination of human
intervention -- a shortening of the chain of command -- and
the reduction of remaining people to unskilled routine and
closely regulated tasks. It is no surprise, then, that AF
development of NC involved no worker or union participation
(NC files MIT). The means of all this was <u>modern methods</u>,
numerical control, i.e., the translation of part specifications into mathematical information which could be fed directly by management into a machine without reliance upon the
skills and initiative of the machinist. The full fantasy was
the fully automatic computer controlled factory, still being
pursued by the Air Force Integrated Computer Aided Manufacturing (ICAM) Program. A December, 1980 AF request for proposal reads: "sources are sought which have the experience,
expertise and production base for establishing a Flexible
Manufacturing System for parts. This FMS should be capable
of providing a technically advanced production facility for
the manufacture of aerospace batch manufactured products.
The system shall be capable of automatically handling and
transporting parts, fixtures, and tools, automatically in-
specting part dimensional quality and incoming tool quality;
integrated system control with machinability data analysis;
computer aided process planning and scheduling and other
capabilities that would provide a totally computer integrated
machining facility." The advertisement in <u>Commerce Business
Daily</u> (Dec. 11, 1980) also points out that "extensive sub-
contracting to aerospace and other manufacturers, machine
tool vendors, universities and other technology companies is
expected." All will get caught up in the military quest for
the automatic factory.

Essentially, numerical control is the technical realization of management control envisioned by the directors of the
Ordnance Department back in the 19th Century. Gauges, patterns, jigs and fixtures, process planning, time studies --
over the years all were designed to get the workforce to
perform, manually or with machinery, in a pre-specified way,
machinelike. NC is a giant step in the same direction; here
management has the capacity to bypass the worker and communi-
cate directly to the machine via tapes on direct computer
link. The machine itself can thereafter pace and discipline
the worker. Essentially this transforms skilled batch work
into continuous process, assembly line work. From the military point of view it is the "command performance," supremely
rational, the dream come true. But economically and socially,
it raises as many problems as it solves.

During the 1940's machine tool manufacturers and control engineers were experimenting with many forms of new equipment for metalworking, trying to put to use war-time developments in electronics and servo-control systems. They came up with improved tracer controlled machines, plugboard-type controls, and record-playback control. The latter was an ingenious development whereby a machinist made a first part manually while the motions of the machine were recorded on magnetic tape; thereafter the tape was simply played back to recreate the machine motions and thereby duplicate the part. These technologies were ideally suited for small batch automatic production, where a change in set-up was required for each short run of parts. All of these systems relied, for set-up (programming) and operation, upon the traditional store of machinist skills and were therefore readily accessible to most metalworking enterprises. But, because of the development of NC, they never got very far in either full development or actual use. NC development as we have just seen was dictated by the performance and command objectives of the Air Force, and these other technologies, which could not be used effectively to make highly complex parts and, most important, which relied upon the skills and resources of workers, were thus perceived from the start as anachronistic and primitive. In fact, however, they represented a significant advance on current methods.

NC was the brainchild of John Parsons, a Michigan manufacturer who was trying to meet the demanding (military) specifications for helicopter rotor blade templates. He elaborated his ideas when he saw a proposed design for an integrally stiffened wing section of a Lockheed fighter, and subsequently sold them to the Air Force. The Air Force eventually contracted with MIT to build the first NC milling machine and thereafter went on to underwrite the software development, the promotion, and the procurement of the new technology, a bulk order purchase which finally elicited the sustained interest of machine tool and electronic control manufacturers. It is important to note, as we examine the uniformity system generally, that the industry did not share the Air Force's enthusiasm for the new technology, and for good reason. Although NC was theoretically ideal for complex machining, it was not necessarily ideal for the vast majority of metalworking orders which were not so demanding. NC was also very costly, not only for the hardware but for the software and computers required to calculate endless amounts of information for the machine controls. NC was also notoriously unreliable and the programming involved was excessive and time-consuming.

In contrast to such other technologies as record-playback

an analog system that was programmed by manual direction or
by following the contour of a pattern, there was no need for
computers, programmers, or excessive training of personnel.
In addition, the programming was right the first time. So,
in terms of manufacturing needs of the metalworking industry,
it would have been rational to proceed with both technologies,
the one for the bulk of metalworking operations, the other
(NC) for subsidized military work. But, the needs of the Air
Force proved hegemonic. When the Air Force gave the signal
for the development of NC and guaranteed lucrative returns
for machine tool and control manufacturers everyone jumped
aboard. All industrial and technical efforts were geared to
meet Air Force specifications.

Other developments which might have proved more accessible, more practical, and more economical for the metalworking industry as a whole were abandoned. The Air Force wanted
highly sophisticated 5 axis machines and a complex, expensive
software system to go with them (the APT system). It enforced their use through the contract system. Machine manufacturers meanwhile concentrated upon the most expensive designs, confident that for their subsidized customers in the
military aerospace industry cost was not a factor.

Performance, command, modern methods: it all made perfect sense for the Air Force. But what were the economic
and social costs? First, some very promising technical possibilities were foreclosed in the wake of the rush to NC.
Second, because of the great expense of the machinery that
was manufactured and the overhead requirements of the programming system, NC was very slow to diffuse into the metalworking industry. Third, the contract system fostered the
larger shops which could underwrite the expense of NC and
APT. In the vast majority of metalworking establishments,
there was no gain from the technical advances in automation
until the 1970's. Fourth, the commercial competitiveness of
U.S. machine manufacturers was undermined.

In April 1979 at the hearings of the House of Representatives Committee on Science and Technology, Congressman Ritter
observed that Japan and Germany invested in machinery for
commercial use rather than military. Predictably, Presidential Science Advisor Frank Press assured the Congressman that
Defense expenditures "spill over" into commercial use. But
Representative Ritter was on to something quite significant.
While U.S. manufacturers were concentrating on highly sophisticated machinery and the APT software system, Japanese and
German manufacturers emphasized cheapness, accessibility and
simplicity in their machine designs and software systems.
The result is painfully obvious: in 1978 the U.S. became a

net importer of machine tools for the first time since the
19th century. And we still can't compete.

For workers, including technical as well as production
personnel, modernization orchestrated according to Air Force
objectives has been disastrous, marked by deskilling, downgrading, routinization, and powerlessness. Autonomy and initiative are giving way to precisely prescribed tasks and
computer monitoring and supervision. This is happening even
though the latest generations of NC machines, equipped with
microprocessors at the machine, now make it possible as
never before for the operator to program and edit at the
machine and to regain control over more sophisticated technology. The technology is rarely used that way, especially
in military-oriented plants. There the trend is rather to
integrate these CNC machines into a larger DNC network under
central command. (At the factory in Kongsberg, Norway, for
example, workers have successfully struggled to regain control over the editing of machines -- except for those who
work on the military F16.) Again, a technical possibility
that might mean lower costs, higher quality and better working conditions is foreclosed by military imperatives. Unions
are being seriously weakened by the new systems and military
strategies. The military requirement of "strategic decen-
tralization" of plants, confronts the unions as runaway
shops subsidized by the state. The military demand for interchangeability and communication networks appears to the
union as satellite-linked duplicate plants that undermine
the power of the strike.

The exaggerated emphasis upon capital intensive methods
and automation, as I have already noted, decreases system reliability (an effect perhaps most obvious in the military
itself) while at the same time eliminating irreplaceable
human skills -- a trend John Parsons himself, the inventor
of NC, finds insane and shortsighted. (Parsons was trained
in manufacturing by an all-around Swedish machinist, precisely the type of people being lost.) Finally, the military
imperatives contribute to dislocation and displacement and
ultimately to structural unemployment -- the very thing the
Luddites were fighting 170 years ago when they helped us win
the War of 1812. This ultimate social cost is now being en-
dured by workers everywhere, invisibly and silently. But
the low profile of this social cost will not last long, once
it becomes obvious to all of us that there is simply no place
for these people to go -- no farms, no factories, no offices.
The faith in the inevitable new industry that will absorb
them rings hollow. Even the computer and control industries
are themselves undergoing automation. Meanwhile, the Air
Force ICAM Project proceeds. Recently, it should be noted,

the Air Force offered a contract for a study of the social
implications of integrated computer-aided manufacture. But
this is no cause for rejoicing. The contract went to Boeing,
one of the major users of the latest automated technology.

Conclusions

It should now be obvious that the military has played a
central role in industrial development and that this role has
left an indelible imprint on that development, the imprint of
performance, command, and modern methods. The three examples
suggest that, while the military influence has not been all
bad, neither has it been an unmixed blessing. They suggest
rather that we must take a closer look at what is happening
under the military aegis. The uniformity system of the Ordnance Department might appear to us as the epitome of progress, but perhaps that is because the people who experienced the disruption of their lives are all dead and gone, their
trials forgotten. To what degree was the system really rational at the time, and what were its social costs? On whose
behalf ought the government to foster technological development? Progress for whom? Containerization raises similar
questions, only here the survivors are still around to haunt
us. What exactly are the presumed economic benefits and
what have been the social costs? Again, progress for whom
and for what? Finally, the computer revolution in manufacturing: what role has the military played in undermining the
competitive viability of U.S. industry? How has it promoted
industrial concentration? How has it contributed to the deskilling of workers and the degrading of working conditions,
the unreliability of our productive plant, the intensifica-
tion of management power and control at the expense of
workers and unions? And, perhaps most crucial, to what extent has it created a yet-to-be-reckoned with structural unemployment, our own twentieth century "world turned upside
down" to borrow Christopher Hill's phrase. Again, what kind
of progress are we talking about here, and progress for whom?

"Performance," "command," "modern methods," these words
do not appear in the U.S. Constitution nor are the subtle yet
profound and pervasive transformations they imply ever voted
upon. The role of the military in shaping our technologies,
our productive activities, our social organizations, the
power relations between us -- in short, in shaping our lives
-- has gone relatively unnoticed and unrecorded. It is time
we gave the matter some serious attention, subjected it to
critical scrutiny, brought it under democratic control. It
is time we began to answer the questions: what kind of progress do we want? What kind of progress can we, as a society
afford?

References

1. United States Air Force, <u>Modern Manufacturing: A Com-
    mand Performance</u> (1965).

2. Smith, M. R., "Military Enterprise and the Innovative
    Process," in Mayer, O. and R. C. Post, <u>The American
    System of Manufacturers</u> (forthcoming).

3. Ibid.

4. Weir, S., "Effects of Containerization on Longshoremen,"
    (U.S. Department of Labor, 1977); Mills, H., "Mechaniza-
    tion of the San Francisco Waterfront" in Zimbalist, A.,
    <u>Case Studies on the Labor Process</u> (New York: Monthly
    Review Press, 1979); Fairly, L., "ILWU-PMA Mechanization
    and Modernization Agreement," (U.S. Department of Labor,
    Labor-Management Services Administration).

5. <u>Op. Cit</u>., H. Mills.

6. Noble, D., "Social Choice in Machine Design," <u>op. cit</u>.,
    in Zimbalist, A.

5. Organized Labor and Economic Conversion

Along with the rest of America'a working men and women, scientists and engineers make up the human component of the nation's progress and prosperity. All contribute to the production from which the nation's power and profits are derived. Scientists conceive and engineers design but it is the skill of America's workforce that transforms cold, unformed metal into sophisticated systems capable of traversing the universe.

Historically, scientists and engineers have tended to hold themselves aloof from working people -- and especially from trade unions. Most scientists and engineers earn their living in exactly the same way as do men and women on the production lines. They trade their skills for cash. Yet a wide chasm of cultural, educational and communications influences divide one group from the other. The barriers of class and caste that isolate scientists and engineers from the rest of the work force are not merely accidental. They have been erected and are maintained for a purpose -- to make it harder for scientists and engineers to unite with workers in challenging the prerogatives, privileges and power of big business.

After all, we -- scientists, technicians, engineers and workers -- are merely employees. As a rule, we aren't entrusted with broad decison-making powers. The big picture -- the overview of our respective projects and production -- is not, we are told, ours to worry about. For the division of labor has made specialists of us all, to the point of overspecialization.

Given the incredible decline of our current political economy and its industrial base, it is time the scientific, engineering and trade union communities coalesce to inject our creative and pragmatic expertise into the decision-making

processes at all policy levels -- in the academic, industrial
and political spheres. We cannot do this for the benefit of
humanity unless we have a vision of society as it should be.

It seems clear to me that we know at least as much as do
our current managers and policy makers about what it takes
to create a peaceful, full employment economy, consistent
with democratic political values. Corporate profits need
not take such precedence over human concerns in the economic
and political decisions of our society. If scientists and
engineers had joined with workers in demanding decision-making powers in the past, it is hard for me to believe that
America would now be suffering such a devasting deterioration
of its political economic base. Government could have been
compelled to give a higher priority to peace, full employment
and price stability than to sabre rattling and financial profits.

I find it hard to imagine, for example, that any group
of scientists, engineers and trade unionists could match the
poor performance of management in the steel, rail, auto and
shipbuilding industries. When those who have recently cap-
tured control of the Federal government now talk about running it like a business, I have to ask -- which business?
Chrysler? Lockheed? U.S. Steel? The Pennsylvania Railroad?
As a result of their own greed and economic myopia, these
corporations, and far too many others, can no longer meet a
payroll. They can't compete in world markets. They survive
only by running to the government for subsidies and handouts.
But ironically they are always the most strident in demanding
free enterprise, supply, demand and the mystical free market
for America's working men and women.

It is equally hard to imagine that scientists and workers would opt for and aggressively pursue an exploitive foreign trade policy that requires an interventionist military
policy to make it work. (Come to think of it, where is the
logic in a system that perpetually prepares for war on a declining industrial base?) It is also hard to imagine that
scientists and workers would permit this country to continue
to be pronged on the twin horns of import dependency and
cartelized prices, without a full scale commitment to safe
energy from renewable sources. This commitment to safe
energy from renewable sources would seem a much wiser policy
than a national commitment, or for that matter a corporate
commitment to the health and cost-maximizing hazards of the
nuclear power path.

American business is even now sowing the seeds of an
economic whirlwind by ignoring the damage being inflicted on
humans, communities and the economy by the accelerating

application of robotics on the assembly line and microelectronic processes in service industries. Robotization goes far beyond automation. It may well not simply depopulate assembly lines, banks and offices, but laboratories, drafting rooms and design studios as well.

Just as war is too important to be left to the generals, corporate policy is too important to be left to multinational conglomerates.

If we are going to change the heading of our current collision course, then we -- the people who design, invent, manufacture, assemble and produce the nation's Gross National Product -- are going to have to get involved in decision-making processes at policy making levels, where they count -- in the private sector and the public sector.

Economic conversion, as we have known it over the years, affords us an opportunity to explore the possibilities of changing our political economy.

Since military production is the nearest approximation to a socialized industry we have, economic conversion permits us to play with fundamental concepts, such as economic planning, at national, local or regional and plant levels; economic conversion lets us theorize about social accountability in the production process; it enables us to manipulate human and capital resources in a context other than profit maximization; it gives us the methodology to canvass and survey unmet national needs, and to design a system that will marry loose or inefficiently employed resources, to fulfillment of those needs.

Economic conversion affords us an opportunity to exercise our pragmatic skills in the redesign of obsolete and unneeded tools, equipment and workplaces, while it employs our imaginative talents in the creation of alternative socially useful products.

In the machinists union, we have taken a very practical approach to economic conversion. We've never called for the wholesale dismantling of the war machine, or sudden and abrupt halts in military production.

We've simply said that whenever, wherever and for whatever reason, military production terminates, or is transferred from one locale to another, then an economic conversion plan ought to be implemented in the impacted facility and community to replace the lost economic activity and vitality, with an eye toward socially useful production.

On the legislative front, we broke the comprehensive conversion bill into three essential elements: advance notice, community and business alternative production planning grants, and income maintenance and health insurance benefits for displaced workers. [Editor's Note: This refers to the Defense Economic Adjustment Act; see Appendix A, pp. 45-60.] In 1979 advance notification and the planning grants were put into the McKinney Amendment to the Economic Development Act; worker protections, into the Dodd Amendment to the Economic Development Act. Tacked on to the Economic Development Act, the Dodd and McKinney Amendments sailed through the House of Representatives in Congress on a voice vote. It was amazing how much sense Economic Conversion made to even fiscal conservatives and big defense spenders, especially those from the Northeast and Great Lakes industrial regions.

But in the Senate, the Pentagon opposed us, and our contractor employees ducked the issue as a group while individually opposing us. Opposition also came from the Chair of the Armed Services Committee and the Chair of the Budget Committee. That all happened at about the same time of the Iranian Crisis, the Soviet invasion of Afghanistan, the demise of the SALT II Treaty and the Carter Administration's decision to increase military spending by quantum leaps.

In addition, the Economic Development Act itself became embroiled in a feud between the House and Senate and between the House and White House. Traditionally, it had been the logrolling, public works pork barrel bill -- a leadpipe cinch to go through Congress. But a substitute was found for it in the last Congress. That was the Omnibus Energy bill, which gave away billions to energy corporations for everything from synfuels to windmills. And the energy giveaway was tacked onto renewal of the Defense Production Act. The House-Senate Conference Committee, which had jurisdiction, never did report an Economic Development bill, so the Dodd and McKinney Economic Conversion Amendments died with the 96th Congress.

With the current Right Wing tilt in Congress, particularly in the Senate, and with the Reagan Administration determined to dramatically increase military spending, chances for present passage of Economic Conversion legislation look poor. However, this will surely not end the effort to work toward policy alternatives to more and more war production. Indeed we are just getting started. The Machinists Union believes that as knowledge and understanding of economic conversion grows, so will support -- especially in the engineering and scientific communities.

When the economy crashes upon millions of working men and women, as any economy tailored to the greed of corporate power inevitably must, we intend to be ready. This means we are refining, improving and expanding our legislative model for economic conversion. In fact, with the help of friends in the engineering, scientific, professional and academic communities, we are moving beyond the concept of simple economic conversion.

When big business economic policies have impoverished enough of America's working men and women, we intend to be ready with a comprehensive program of economic reconstruction. And by reconstruction we are not limiting ourselves to the kind of "reindustrialization" proposals that have been bruited about by others recently.

Economic reconstruction, unlike "reindustrialization," does not mean merely more tax breaks for the wealthy and more subsidies for big business. In addition to breaking the bonds of economic necessity that now keep so much of the work force captive to war production, the concept of economic reconstruction extends to the far greater and more fruitful task of rebuilding America. Economic reconstruction means building our inner cities through a domestic Marshall Plan that encourages people at the local government and neighborhood levels to design and develop economic enterprises of their own. It is keyed to the Federal Financing Bank, an off-budget office in the Treasury Department, and does not, I emphasize, contemplate the creation or need for more federal bureaucracy, red tape or guidelines.

Let it be clearly understood that, in saying this, we are not abandoning the concept of economic conversion. It continues to have our full support. We are simply incorporating it under the broader umbrella of comprehensive economic reconstruction.

6. The Trade Union Stake in Economic Conversion

Like other Americans, many trade unionists have viewed military economy as a source of income and jobs. But the effects of a long-enduring war economy include inflation and unemployment that more than offset, for all working people, the income and employment gains of those paid by the military.

For trade unionists and others doing production work, the unemployment effect of war economy is destructive. When managers close factories, production employment ends. Meanwhile, firms can and do continue -- with production done in other countries. This can mean continued jobs for U.S. financial, administrative, and sales staffs, but no U.S.-based work for engineers and production workers. Thus, the financial well-being of a firm does not necessarily include employment for U.S. producers.

The military economy sector spans 20,000 industrial firms in which a major part of production is on Pentagon order. Also, there are 100,000 sub-contractors. These firms have special qualities: unlike the typical civilian product firms, they maximize costs and offset this by maximizing subsidies from the Federal government. This means the establishment of internal, managerial, engineering, and allied practices within the firms, specified by the Pentagon, that press relentlessly towards enlarging costs.[2] No component of industrial cost is exempt from this process.[1] For example, by 1972 in all U.S. manufacturing there were 42 administrative and related employees per 100 production workers. In the main Pentagon-serving industries the ratio was 69 per 100.

As this process proceeds within the military economy, it infects civilian industry as well.[7] Administrative and production practices prescribed for military industry by the

Table 1.   Examples of jobs lost in depleted U.S. industries because of non-competitiveness

Industry	U.S. Jobs Replaced by Imports		U.S. Jobs Lost
	1964	1972	1976
Men's and Boy's Suits & Coats	800	7,100	12,141
Men's and Boy's Shirts & Nightwear	4,000	18,200	18,841
Children's Outwear	15,300	31,700	43,250
Wood Products	4,800	9,800	47,271
Furniture & Fixtures	2,600	11,900	157,823
Rubber & Plastics Footwear	4,100	13,300	7,490
Men & Women's Footwear	6,500	32,600	44,059
Fine Earthware Food Utensils	2,000	5,600	5,760
Pottery Products	2,100	5,100	14,119
Fabricated Metal Products	2,900	7,200	35,457
Textile Machinery	3,500	16,400	10,436
General Industrial Machinery	3,400	6,700	21,275
Typewriters & Office Machines	3,400	17,400	17,762
Calculating & Accounting Machines	1,300	5,300	5,605
Sewing Machines	3,600	5,200	6,034
Current Carrying Wiring Devices	900	6,100	8,241
Radio & TV Receiving Sets	7,600	37,700	36,668
Radio & TV Communication Equipment	2,300	9,700	38,062
Semiconductors	700	11,800	24,641
Motor Vehicles, Bodies & Parts	13,700	95,900	115,694
Aircraft Equipment	3,500	10,400	6,236
Motorcycles, Bicycles & Parts	4,500	28,300	11,867
Measuring, Controlling Devices	400	7,800	9,399
Watches, Clocks & Watchcases	4,100	7,100	13,664
Games, Toys, Children's Vehicles	2,900	6,600	6,808
Sporting & Athletic Goods	2,500	8,100	8,282

Estimating method: (Imports ÷ Value of Shipments from U.S. factories) x Total Employees of the Industry = Estimate of U.S. employment lost owing to imports.

*Only industries with an estimated job loss of 5,000 or more by 1972 were included here.

Pentagon are adopted by civilian divisions of the same firms
(e.g. - why operate two accounting systems?). Equipment and
raw materials for which lavish prices are paid by military
users are often kindred to materials and equipment used in
civilian firms. The cost-maximizing of the military economy
becomes a model for cost and price increases for civilian
operation as well.

As people transfer from military to civilian firms (or
from military to civilian parts of the same firm) they carry
with them the ways of performing their jobs that have been
acceptable and well regarded in the service of the Pentagon.
Thereby, work practices that are part of the cost-maximizing
process get transferred to civilian type operations. The
same occurs on the management side.

In firms partly devoted to serving the military there is
a requirement from compliance with Pentagon regulations.
Civilian divisions of the same firm can come under pressure
to follow suit owing to differences between the firm's traditional requirements and the specifications of the Department of Defense. Typically, the Pentagon has a dispropor-
tionate influence, since it is an unusually large customer.
Therefore its requirements carry considerably more weight
than its portion of the firm's business may imply. By such
means, cost-maximizing practices established directly under
Pentagon regulations in the military-serving firms extend
their cost and price increasing operation to the civilian
economy.

The diversion of R&D and capital resources from civilian
economy has caused industries to fall behind in product design, production methods and productivity of labor and capital. Many important industries have become depleted -- unable to serve their market. There is not much in the U.S.
to compare with the high-speed mass transit systems of Japan,
Germany, Sweden, or France. So imports are increasingly the
vogue in steel, automobile, railroad equipment, consumer
electronics, quality optics, shoes, textiles -- to name a
few that head the list. When such U.S. industries become
incompetent relative to foreign-based firms, the result is
the massive growth of imports to serve the U.S. market.
Opportunity for productive livelihood for Americans is reduced, whether the ownership of the facilities abroad is U.S.
or foreign.

In Table 1 are shown estimates of employment foregone
in the United States in a sample of 26 manufacturing industries as a consequence of growing non-competitiveness. Employment foregone is estimated by applying to the total

number of people employed in an industry the ratio of imports
to the "value of shipments" from the factories of each industry.
(1964 is the last year before the military escalation in
Vietnam.)

In the radio and TV equipment industry, shoe manufacturing, clothing manufacturing, and the automobile industry,
the effects are large enough to account for the important
concentration of unemployment that has appeared in the cities
and states that have long had many factories in these industries. The steel industry is the latest one to show sharp
employment loss. For example, from August to December 1977,
20,000 production worker, technician and administrative jobs
were ended in the U.S. steel industry.

The erosion of U.S. employment opportunities in many
industries has not been halted by the cheapening of the relative price of U.S. labor, compared with foreign labor. That
was one result of the decline in the value of the dollar in
relation to other currencies from 1972 on. While certain industries (like equipment for power plants) have enjoyed re-
newed export markets as a result of that development, the
employment decay in the largest number of industries shown
here has been continuing. Once industrial investments are
made abroad, for example, the plant, equipment, and the many
investments in staffing factories become assets to the investors, and there is pressure on management to continue their
use. This solidifies the employment loss in the U.S.

As price inflation proceeds in the machinery producing
industries, this has a special set of effects both for employment there and, indirectly as well, in the whole range of
machinery-using industries. One of the root processes in a
cost-minimizing industrial economy is the effect of the rise
in the wages of labor, in greater degree than the prices of
machinery. This makes the purchase of machinery a more attractive option to the cost-minimizing employer. However,
when machinery prices increase as much or more rapidly than
the wages of labor, the purchase of new production equipment
becomes an unattractive option to a cost-minimizing employer.
This lowers employment levels within the machinery-producing
industries.

But the consequences of making new equipment economically unattractive affect the rest of the industrial system as
well. For as new machinery is not purchased, and as the
capital stock of manufacturing industry ages, the result is
a lessened rate of productivity growth, less ability to offset cost increases, and consequent growth of price non-competitiveness. Thereby, unemployment effects are multiplied
throughout the industrial system.

Crucial evidence on the extent of this development comes from the McGraw-Hill Company's 1973 inventory of machine tools in U.S. industry. They reported on 29 October, 1973 (American Machinist, page 143) that by 1973 67% of machine tools in use in U.S. industry were ten years old or over. This was the oldest stock of metal-working machinery in any industrial country. The U.S. rate of productivity growth was thus depressed leading to growing non-competiveness and unemployment in the manufacturing industries.

In addition, as holders of capital seek opportunities for investment they discover that civilian economic growth proceeds more rapidly in countries that do not have a permanent war economy. During the 1960's U.S. investors discovered better prospects abroad, especially in Western Europe and in Canada. Accordingly, about $47,000,000,000 of direct foreign investment was carried out by Americans during the 1960's. This accounted for the equivalent transfer abroad of 3 to 4 million manufacturing and allied jobs.[3]

But, there are other unemployment generating effects. In conventional wisdom one way to diminish inflation is to retard investment and other spending by raising the interest rate, thereby making it more costly to borrow money. But as this is done, and as new investment and other economic activity is diminished, the result is a reduction in employment opportunity. (Also, such strategies did not eliminate inflation during the 1970's.)

Furthermore, spending for military industry products characteristically generates less direct employment than do many kinds of civilian expenditure. Dr. Roger Bezdek, an economist at the Energy Resource and Development Administration, has calculated the direct job effect from spending $1,000,000,000 in each of the indicated activities. His results are set out in Table 2.

Military production, especially of the more technically ornate sort, is capital-intensive, including major charges for the use of specialized and costly research, testing, and manufacturing facilities. Also, military industry operates with lavish administrative overhead facilities and salaries. A net result of high capital and manpower costs in military economy is less direct employment, compared with civilian economy, per dollar spent.

Military work uses up resources which could have been applied to economic-productive purposes. Bruce Russett of Yale University has estimated the average reduction in major economic sectors that is associated with spending on military economy.[4] Thus, for the period 1939-1968 an average increase

Table 2. Estimates of employment generated by $1 billion federal spending in various activities

Program	Jobs
Military Aerospace	58,000
Army Corp. of Engineers	69,000
Law Enforcement	75,000
Sanitation	78,000
Mass Transit Construction	83,000
Public Housing	84,000
Highway Construction	84,000
Conservation and Recreation	88,000
Welfare Payments	99,000
Social Security	108,000
Education	118,000

Source: G. Adams, The B-1 Bomber: An Analysis of Its Strategic Utility, Cost, Constituency, and Economic Impact, Report of the Council on Economic Priorities, 1976, p. 21.

of one dollar in military spending was associated with reduction in the following areas: Personal consumption (durable, non-durable goods and services) - 42 cents less.
Exports - 9 cents less.
Imports - 2 cents less.
Federal civil purchases - 4 cents less.
State and Local government consumption - 12 cents less.

Military spending removes something from each of these economic areas, with the main effects showing up in less personal consumption and less fixed investment.

Marion Anderson has estimated the net employment effect associated with the classes of economic activity foregone owing to military spending. Her estimate of the negative employment impact of military spending shows an annual average (1968-1972) of 844,000 jobs foregone.[5]

The fiscal crisis in many U.S. cities is a derived effect of the transfer of capital and purchasing power, via federal taxes and spending, to the centers of military bases and industry. So the cities of the northeast and the midwest have been hardest hit by the cumulative effect of money withdrawn to serve the military economy.[6]

The combined direct effects of capital invested abroad during the 1960 decade and the employment that is foregone

in civilian economy owing to military spending has been in
the range of not less than 3,500,000 to 4,500,000 jobs foregone in recent years. If one assumes a modest multiplier
effect, then a doubling of these estimates is in order. This
brings the civilian unemployment effect associated with the
sustained military economy of the U.S. to the range of
7,000,000 to 9,000,000 jobs.

There is more industrial unemployment to come. It is
possible to anticipate the continuation of the depletion process and to forecast at least a part of the location and the
magnitude of its effects. One device for accomplishing this
is through analysis of an unusual body of data made available
to the public by the initiative of Dr. Michael Boretsky, a
senior economic analyst at the U.S. Department of Commerce.
The U.S. Bureau of the Census, which prepares the Census of
Manufacturers, calculated for each factory ("establishment")
of selected industries the "value added by manufacture" per
employee. This is a productivity measure where the output
is represented by the money value of shipments minus purchased materials, containers, and power. The factories of each
industry were then ranked according to their productivity
level. The Bureau then calculated the ratio between the
average productivity of the top quartile of factories in each
industry and the average productivity for the industry.
These figures appear in the first column of Table 3. For
example, for 1967 in the Blast Furnaces and Steel Mills
(industry No. 3312) the 1.5 figure means that the top quartile of factories of that industry, in terms of productivity,
were 1.5 times as efficient as the average for the industry.

Similarly, reading across and to the right, the next
column shows the ratio of the top quartile to the lowest
quartile of that industry. By 1967 the factories in the top
quartile of the steel industry were 2.3 times as productive
as the lowest quartile.

Clearly, the lowest quartile of the iron and steel and
other industries is the least competent part in terms of cost
and price competiveness. The factories of this lowest quartile in each industry are the first to go when firms decide
to shut down non-competitive divisions. Thus, the factories
that were shut down in seven states from August to November
1977 in the iron and steel industry were surely of that class.

Following this reasoning, I have reckoned that the lowest quartile of factories in each of the identified industries is the section of greatest weakness and the first likely to suffer unemployment from the discovery by management
that divisions of their firm are no longer cost and price-
competitive. Accordingly, I show on the right hand of Table 3

Table 3. Disparities in the level of productivity within selected U.S. manufacturing industries

SIC Code*	Ratio of value-added/ employee in 25 % highest productivity establishments (plants), to the industry average of the industry 1967	Ratio of value-added/ employee in 25 % highest productivity establishments, to the value-added/ employee in 25 % worst performing establishments 1967	Total Employees 1974 (000)	Estimated no. employees in 25 % lowest productivity establishments (25 % of Total employees)
2211	1.4	1.9	108.5 ('75)	27,100
2621	1.4	2.2	130.4	32,600
2812	2.3	3.2	13.7	3,400
2821	1.8	3.6	57.7	14,400
2911	1.5	4.8	102.9	25,700
3211	1.2	2.4	21.5	5,100
3312	1.5	2.3	518.0	129,500
3323	1.5	1.8	53.3 ('75)	13,300
3334	1.1	1.7	25.3 ('75)	6,300
3391	1.4	1.9	39.4	9,800
3461	1.3	1.7	101.1	25,200
3519	1.6	2.3	80.8	20,200
3522	1.4	2.1	130.8 ('75)	32,700
3541	1.3	1.9	62.8	15,700
3561	1.6	2.1	63.9	13,500
3621	1.4	1.8	100.2	25,000
3632	1.4	1.6	32.7	8,200

Table 3, continued

SIC Code* average of the industry	Ratio of value-added/employee in 25 % highest productivity establishments (plants), to the average of the industry 1967	Ratio of value-added/employee in 25 % highest productivity establishments, to the value-added/employee in 25 % worst performing establishments 1967	Total Employees 1974 (000)	Estimated no. employees in 25 % lowest productivity establishments (25 % of Total employees)
3717	1.4	2.5	889.0 ('73)	222,200
3722	1.4	1.8	108.0 ('75)	27,000
Average	1.5	2.4		Total 656,900

*2211 Broad woven fabric mills, cotton
2621 Paper mills, except building paper mills
2812 Alkalies & chlorine
2821 Plastics materials & resins
2911 Petroleum refining
3211 Flat glass
3312 Blast furnaces & steel mills
3323 Steel foundries
3334 Primary products of aluminum
3391 Iron & steel forgings
3461 Metal stampings
3519 Internal combustion engines, n.e.c.
3522 Farm machinery & equipment
3541 Machine tools, metal cutting
3561 Pumps & compressors
3621 Motors & generators
3632 Household refrigerators & freezers
3717 Motor vehicles & parts
3722 Aircraft engines & parts

Sources: Productivity data, M. Boretsky, U.S. Technology: Trends and Policy Issues, U.S. Dept. of Commerce, Oct. 1973. Based on special tabulations of census schedules in regular census years by the Dept. of Commerce, Bureau of the Census; U.S. Bureau of the Census, Annual Survey of Manufacturers, for 1974 and 1975, Motor Vehicles, 1973, from U.S. Statistical Abstract for 1977, p. 773.

Table 4. Illustrative new programs or major expansions
of existing federal civilian programs, fiscal year 1972
(derived from proposals of task forces and study groups)

Program	Hypothetical Expenditures (billions of dollars)
Total Expenditures	39.7
Education	7.0
Preschool	1.0
Elementary & Secondary	2.5
Higher	3.0
Vocational	.5
Health	3.8
Kiddie-care	.5
Medicare for Disabled	1.8
Comprehensive Health Centers	1.0
Hospital Construction & Modernization	.5
Nutrition	1.0
Community Service Programs	.8
Jobs & Manpower	2.5
Public Jobs	1.8
Manpower Development Training Act	.5
Employment Service	.2
Social Security & Income Support	9.5
Unemployment Insurance	2.0
Public Assistance	4.0
Social Security Improvements	3.5
Veterans	.3
Economic, Area, & Other Special Development Programs	2.2
Entrepreneurial Aid	.5
Area Redevelopment	.5
Rural Development	1.0
Indian Assistance	.2
Crime, Delinquency, & Riots	1.0
Violence & Riot Prevention	.1
Safe Streets Programs	.3
Rehabilitation of Offenders & Deliquents	.3
Prevention of Delinquency & Crime by Special Measures for Delinquency-prone Youth	.3
Quality of Environment	1.7
Air Pollution Prevention & Control	.1

Table 4, continued

Program	Hypothetical Expenditures (billions of dollars)
Public Water Supply Construction Programs	.3
Water Pollution Control & Sewage Treatment	1.0
Solid Waste Disposal	.1
Natural Beautification, Environmental Protection, & Recreational Development	.2
Natural Resource Development & Utilization	1.4
Land & Forest Conservation	.2
Water Resources & Related Programs	.5
Mineral & Energy (excluding Hydroelectric Development)	.2
Natural Environmental Development	.5
Urban Development	5.5
New Cities	.5
Land Acquisition & Financial Planning (Suburban)	.5
Urban Mass Transportation	.5
Model Cities	2.0
Other Urban Facilities & Renewal	2.0
Transportation	1.0
Airway & Airport Modernization	.4
Rapid Interurban Ground Transit	.1
Modernization of Merchant Marine	.2
Motor Vehicle & Transportation Safety Research & Safety Grants	.3
Science & Space Exploration	1.0
Post-Apollo Space Program	.5
Scientific Research in Oceanography Communications, Social & Behavioral Sciences, & Natural Sciences	.5
Foreign Economic Aid	1.0

Source: "Report to the President from the Cabinet Coordinating Committee on Economic Planning for the End of Vietnam Hostilities," in Economic Report of the President, transmitted to the Congress January 1969. The Report includes an explanation of the content of the program categories.

the total number of employees in each industry as of 1974-75.
In the last column, at the right I show numbers comprising
25% of each industry's workers, managers, and technicians.
These groups in the least productive quartile of each industry
will very likely be the first to be rendered unemployed as the
process of industrial depletion continues in the United States.

By this reckoning, 656,000 employees will be in the
first wave of job loss in these industries during the next
period. There has been no attempt just yet to estimate the
speed of these processes within each industry. But the record of the 1960's and the 1970's shows that the sort of des-
truction of opportunity for livelihood that is defined here
can be anticipated within the next five-ten years.

New capital outlays of this size, sustained and planned in advance, are equivalent to a major list of new markets
for which industrial firms can bid and in relation to which
many people could plan new job opportunities. The 1969 agenda can be updated and the civilian investment planning can be
extended to include not only federal, but also state, county,
city enterprise, and regional (including ex-military base)
planning.

A further illustration of new capital spending possibilities is the schedule of Public Facility Needs prepared in
1966 for the Joint Economic Committee (Table 4).

When realistic plans for major capital outlays to repair
the long depletion of the U.S. economy are prepared and published by all these parties, the total activity will probably
far exceed the capacity of the U.S. economy. The existence
of such investment plans will give confidence in the work-
ability of economic futures in place of those to be obtained
from military industry and military bases. The translation
from new investment to jobs can be reasonably estimated:
assuming $12,000 as the average cost of a man-year, then $50
billion generates, directly 4,500,000 jobs. To allow con-
servatively for multiplier effects, double that figure.

These effects of a durable war economy in producing inflation and unemployment are destructive of the basic requirement of every economy: that it organize people to perform the useful work that is indispensable for continued
life. A community must produce in order to live. As production is foregone in favor of money-making by other means,
then opportunity for livelihood is closed off for people in
the productive occupations. That is why trade unionists
have a special stake in competent planning for economic conversion to a civilian alternative to a military-oriented
economy.

References

1. For a detailed "insider's view" of this process see
    Fox, J. R., Arming America (Cambridge: Harvard Uni-
    versity Press, 1974).

2. Fitzgerald, A. E., The High Priests of Waste (New
    York: W. W. Norton, 1972), pp. 18-19 and variously
    throughout the text.

3. Melman, S., The Permanent War Economy (New York:
    Simon & Shuster, 1974), pp. 97-104; P. G. Musgrave,
    "Direct Investment Abroad and the Multinationals:
    Effects on the United States Economy," Subcommittee
    on Multinational Corporations, Committee on Foreign
    Relations, United States Senate, U.S. Government
    Printing Office, August, 1975, pg. 14

4. Russett, B. M., What Price Vigilance: The Burdens
    of National Defense (New Haven: Yale University Press,
    1970), pp. 140-141.

5. Anderson, M., The Empty Pork Barrel, Public Interest
    Research Group in Michigan (615 E. Michigan Ave.,
    Lansing, Michigan 48933) April 1975.

6. "Federal Spending: The North's Loss is the Sunbelt's
    Gain," National Journal, June 26, 1976; J. R. Anderson,
    "The Balance of Military Payments Among States and
    Regions," in Melman, S., ed. The War Economy of the
    United States (New York: St. Martin's Press, 1971).

7. The Lucas Aerospace Corporate Plan for Transition to Socially Useful Production

Background

Lucas Industries is a vast and complex organization with design, development, manufacturing, sales and service activities in the automotive, aerospace and industrial sectors of the economy.

The Company, which was formed in 1877, now has 80,000 employees and an annual turnover of approximately £300,000,000 and capital investment of £110,000,000.

A discernible feature of the Company's mode of operation during the past few years has been to shift large quantities of capital, resources and technological know-how into overseas activities. This raises a whole host of fundamental, political, economic and industrial questions, as is the case with the operation of any multinational corporation. It is not the purpose of the Corporate Plan to analyze these. Suffice to say that this tendency is causing deep-rooted concern among large sections of Lucas employees, and they will clearly have to consider appropriate means of defining themselves from the likely repercussions of these developments. These views and anxieties are reflected in the Aerospace Division.

Lucas Industries hold a monopoly, or near monopoly position, in respect of a number of product ranges both in the United Kingdom and in Europe. However the present economic crisis is having serious repercussions within Lucas Industries. The Company is attempting to shed large sections of labour in some of its plants. There has been a serious cut in the living standards of all Lucas workers both by hand and brain since 1972. The attitude of the Company to its employees and society at large is however no worse than that of its

international competitors and it is certainly better than
some of them. However, a sophisticated industrial relations
set up and a relatively elaborate network of consultative
devices simply provide a thin veneer of concern.

The five years from 1964 to 1969 saw very rapid monopol-
ization of large sections of British Industry and the emer-
gence of massive corporations such as British Leyland and
GEC. This process was actively supported by the government,
which, in many instances, was providing the tax payers money
to lubricate this process. Within Mr. Wilson's philosophical
framework of "the white heat of technological change" many
thousands of highly skilled workers found that the consequence of the "White Heat" market economy was that it simply
burned up their jobs and gave rise to large scale structural
unemployment. The "logic" of the market economies and rationalization programmes in these vast corporations resulted
in the illogical growth of the unemployment queue with all
the degradation and suffering and loss of economic activity
of hundreds of thousands of highly skilled men and women.

The Weinstock empire, that is GEC, was the pacemaker
in this development. The workforce was reduced from 260,000
to 200,000 while during the same period the profits went up
from £75,000,000 to £108,000,000 per annum. Thus while it
was profitable for Weinstock to cut his workforce, society at
large had to pay the price, first in social security payments
for those involved and second in the loss of productive capacity which these people could have made available to the
economy of the nation as a whole. Weinstock's attitude to
the workforce, summed up by one of his managers in a statement to the Sunday Times "he takes people and squeezes them
until the pips squeak" was seen as some kind of virtue. Is
this the pinnacle of managerial competence it was held up to be?

When Lucas acquired parts of English Electric in the
process described above, the lessons of the Weinstock esca-
pade were not lost on Lucas workers. It was clear that Lucas
Aerospace, if it were permitted, would embark on a similar
rationalization programme. Strangely enough it was recognition that this attack would be made upon the workforce that
provided the objective circumstances in which the Combine
Committee was formed.

Its formation resulted in the first instance from fear
of layoffs, and the recognition of the need to provide an organization which could fight and protect the right to work.
It was realized from the onset that the Combine Committee
could itself become another bureaucracy and that there were
real dangers in centralizing activities of all factories
through one body. Accordingly a constitution was carefully

worked out and widely discussed at all sites which provided
adequate safeguards.

Development of the Combine Committee, now known as the
Lucas Aerospace and Defence Systems Combine Shop Stewards
Committee, took approximately 4-1/2 years. In its early
stages it lacked cohesion and strength. The Company was, as
a result of this, able to embark on a rationalization programme in which the work force was reduced from 18,000 to the
present 13,000.

Gradually the Combine Committee set up a series of advisory services for its members. These include a pensions
advisory service which has recently negotiated a complex pension structure for manual workers[1] and the campaign for the
election of trustees for the staff pension fund in order that
information could be available as to where this pension fund
money is being invested. The importance of this development
may be judged by the fact that the staff pension fund has
market value of something like £80,000,000 and the works one
£40,000,000 at a time when the capitalization value of Lucas
as a whole on the stock market has been as low as £36,000,000.

Other services included a Science Technology Advisory
Service which provided technical information on the safeguards to be compaigned for when new equipment was being introduced[2] or when health hazards were possibly involved.[3]

The Combine Committee is also a reflection of the growing awareness, of those who work at the point of production,
that the traditional trade union structures based on geographical divisions and organized on a craft basis are incapable
of coping with the new and complex problems of these large
monopolies. However, the Combine Committee should not be
seen as an alternative to the traditional trade union movement; rather it is a logical development from it and compli-
mentary to its aims.

The Combine Committee produces its own four-page illustrated newspaper approximately bi-monthly; 10,000 copies
of this are circulated among the 13,000 manual and staff
workers.

In practice the Combine Committee has become the voice
on a number of subjects for the 13,000 annual and staff-work-
ers who now work throughout Lucas Aerospace abroad.

As has been discussed, Lucas Aerospace, part of the
giant British-based multinational, Lucas Industries, had reduced the workforce from 18,000 to 13,000 between 1970 and
1975. The firm's intentions were to reduce the workforce to

8,000-9,000 within the decade. They have failed because of
good shop stewards' organization, and because of the development of a new type of strategy, the Workers' Plan - called an
Alternative Corporate Plan by the Lucas Aerospace Combine
Shop Stewards Committee.

Lucas, like many other big British companies, was regarded as a sleeping giant in the 1950's and '60's, but was
awakened by the pressures of international competition in the
mid and late '60's. Lucas became a conglomerate. This meant
that Lucas Aerospace expanded greatly in size through acquir-
ing new companies - which were then split up, parts closed
down, reorganized, rationalized, and large numbers of people
laid off.

Shop stewards in Lucas Aerospace felt that they had to
get together in some way to combat the management's divide
and rule tactics. They spent the early 1970's developing a
national combine shop stewards committee, representing workers in all 17 Lucas Aerospace sites, in all 13 trade unions.
During this time the company continued with its closures and
layoffs, despite the imposition by the stewards of various
sorts of industrial action, including strikes and even a
factory occupation at one of the London plants.

Developing the Corporate Plan

In 1974, with a new Labour Government in power which
had a programme to nationalize aerospace and shipbuilding,
the Combine decided to approach Tony Benn, the Industry Minister, to discuss whether nationalization of Lucas Aerospace
could help them to combat closures and layoffs. At a meeting
with Tony Benn in November 1974, it was clear to the Combine
that the Government would not be able to nationalize Lucas
Aerospace as it was only part of the much bigger multinational,
Lucas Industries. The Combine Committee could not therefore rely on this type of government intervention to save
jobs and they started to think of a different strategy, one
which could succeed where occupations, strikes and industrial action could not. They started to think about putting
forward discussion and/or negotiating proposals in the event
of future layoffs which could use their members' skills and
labour in the production of products which the Company was
either dropping or unwilling to make. The Combine Committee
wrote to 180 leading academics and experts in Britain and
elsewhere. They received just three replies. Consequently,
the Combine Committee turned instead to the engineering and
factory floor workforce of Lucas Aerospace itself, asking for
an audit of job skills and equipment available to be undertaken, and for alternative product and production suggestions
that would maintain the flow of work.

They began a careful process of survey and discussion required, among other things, to overcome the initial reluctance of the workforce to venture into areas of decision-making in which they were not accustomed to participating. Soon hundreds of replies came back. These were pooled into about 150 product suggestions, together with proposals for better work organization, for training and retraining, and for different types of markets. Some of the products were not necessarily profitable, but all had some clear social benefit, such as energy-saving equipment, better equipment for public transport and so on. Most of the products were designed for easy maintenance and repair, although quite a few were high technology products, and all of course could be manufactured with existing plant and with the existing workforce, although quite a few products could be built jointly with workers in other firms or industries.

The Combine formed a bargaining position over what they called their "alternative corporate plan," which ran to six 200-page documents.

Given that military and military-related work was a large part of the focus of Lucas Aerospace, and therefore of the occupational experience of the workforce, it was particularly interesting that very few of the product proposals had any sort of military use. There seemed instead to be a clear emphasis on what might be called "socially useful products" and on safety at work and in the community. The workforce had come up with a whole host of product suggestions which seem to have obvious social benefits. The Combine Committee therefore maintained that they were not simply campaigning for the right to work, but for the right to work on socially useful products.

The Combine Committee considered that some of the product proposals might enable Lucas Aerospace to make a conventional profit, but others were not necessarily profitable and the shop stewards hoped that their corporate plan would not simply be a sort of super suggestion scheme for the management. What they were doing was to raise the idea of use value, which of course is the basic way in which companies conventionally view products. That is, products are not viewed in terms of how useful they are, but in terms of amount of money that can be made by the Company by their production and sale.

Firms design products in order to make money, not in order to make products. While this might often create useful products like mousetraps or bicycles or safety helmets, it doesn't necessarily do so. Lucas Aerospace is a major European manufacturer of military aerospace hardware. Indepen-

dent of personal worldviews on international defence or arms
sales, this industry is volatile, job security is low, and
the manufacture of alternative products which clearly meet
unmet social needs might well be a more effective path toward
economic security for the workforce. Workers in Lucas Aerospace apparently hold that view.

The Corporate Plan

It is clearly beyond the scope of the present analysis
to set forth either a comprehensive list of all the 150 proposals contained in the Plan, or even to describe a few of
these proposals in full technical detail. Instead, by way of
illustration[6], we outline several proposals and present a
summarized list of a larger group of the major product proposals included in the Plan.

Oceanics. The ocean beds cover over 70% of the earth's
surface. It is clear that during the coming years there will
be an ever increasing use made of this vast area. Judging by
the irresponsible manner in which human beings have used the
first 30% of the earth's surface the prospect is one which
we view with considerable trepidation.

The exploitation of the ocean bed is likely to take at
least three forms:

1. Exploration and extraction of oil and natural
    gas.
2. Collection of metal bearing nodules.
3. Submarine agriculture.

It has been estimated that 15% of the world's oil is already drawn from coastal waters and this figure will be increased to 33% by 1980. The significance of this in the
United Kingdom has of course been underlined by the work on
North Sea Oil[4]. The scale of this activity may be judged
by the fact that the total capital expenditure in process
industries is forecast to amount to 8.6 billion pounds in
the three years up to the end of 1977. Of this some 40% is
likely to go on North Sea Oil production development.[5]

Five years ago, efforts to interest Mr. Rivett and Mr.
Clifton-Mogg in the possibility of using existing Lucas Aerospace valve technology, and the manufacturing facilities of
the ballscrews to provide a complete valve operating and controlled system were ignored. It is perhaps not surprising
therefore that Sir Fredrick Warner, Chairman of the NEDC process plant working committee, maintains that process plant and
equipment manufacturers are losing out to overseas companies
on much of the North Sea Oil work. He stated in presenting

the NEDC report on 9 June 1975, "I wish we were getting half the business."[6]

Although such valve work would represent only a minor part of the capital investment in such installations it would have been of major significance to Lucas Aerospace. However the real growth area would be in a whole range of automatic and electronically controlled remote equipment. It is easy to envisage a time when all facilities now used in processing and distributing oil are put in the sea bed in vast plants manned by people living in atmospheric conditions, or handled by robots and automatic systems electronically controlled from the shore.[7]

It is significant that Westinghouse and Lockheed are both actively engaged in these fields, and Lockheed is concentrating its efforts on developing subsea working chambers which can be approached by diving bells.[8]

These activities will require a wide range of submersible vehicles which in turn will need generating and actuating systems on board. Lucas Aerospace should be entering into working agreements with the manufacturers of these, in particular Vickers Oceanics. In fact they should consider entering into an agreement with Vickers which would establish the same relationship which they have in the aerospace field with Hawker Siddeley or BAC.

Metal Bearing Nodules

One of the richest sources of mineral resources is the metal bearing nodules to be found on the sea bed. They exist virtually everywhere and are usually 20mm to 40mm in size and average 17% manganese and 11% iron. They also contain considerable quantities of trace elements, of nickel, copper, cobalt and zinc, together with lead and phosphates. By the year 2000 the land sources of some of these metals will have been exhausted, while the marine reserves are enormous. The quantity of copper in nodule form, for example, is 150 times greater than the terrestrial reserves.[9]

Although this field of activity is only in its infancy, three large companies in the United States, including Hughes Tool, have already put $100 million into the project to exploit the seas off California. In Europe, both France and Germany have carried out initial experiments with deep sea retrievers. The initial investment of projects of this kind is likely to be enormous and as a consequence international cooperation is likely to be the pattern. In fact, a spokesman for the German company said "the technical development is so expensive that exploitation of these metal bearing nodules is out of the question for one firm alone, or even a national group of companies. It can only be done by international co-operation as through cross frontier consortia."

Marine Agriculture

During the coming ten years there is likely to be a growing interest in marine agriculture. Products of the sub-aqua farms are likely to range from directly consumable vegetables to those producing by-products which can be pro-cessed on land. This type of farming will require a whole range of special purpose small vehicles to take the "farmers" down to the work areas. There are also likely to be require-ments for a range of submersible vehicles and telechiric machines which could carry out both the sowing and reaping by remote control. It is our view that oceanics provides a very important long-term outlet for Lucas Aerospace as manufactur-ers of complete aircraft systems. We are in a unique posi-tion to provide total systems for the vehicles and equipment which will be required in this field. It would also be a logical point of entry for Lucas Aerospace into the wider and developing field of control systems as a whole. This is likely to be one of the leading growth areas during the com-ing years and a very considerable use of mini-computers and micro-processors are likely to be involved. The predictions are that this will have a profound effect upon the whole nature of our technology during the coming years.[10] This field would also provide a logical framework in which Lucas Aerospace could get involved in micro-processing systems. It is significant that some of Lucas' leading competitors such as Plessey are already making considerable advances in the micro-processor field.

Braking Systems. The increased speed of both road and rail vehicles and the larger payloads which they will carry both of passengers and goods will give rise to stringent braking regulations, during the coming years. This tendency will be further increased by Britain's membership in the EEC. The EEC is now introducing a range of new braking regulations. These specify, not only stopping distances, but call for min-imum standards of braking endurance over a continuous period. In addition, the regulations lay down conditions for "braking balance" between axles in order to prevent a dangerous se-quence of wheel locking.

Many individual EEC countries have, in addition, their own national braking requirements. In France for example, since the mid 1950's auxiliary braking systems have been com-pulsory for coaches operating in mountainous terrain.

A fundamental weakness of normal mechanical brakes is

that when subjected to long braking periods they overheat and the braking linings, at elevated temperatures, tend to temporarily lose their "gripping qualities." This problem can be greatly reduced, if not totally overcome, by using a retarder. A retarder is basically an electromagnetic dynamometer which is usually fitted to the prop shaft between the engine and the back axle. To reduce speed, its coils are excited by an electrical supply coming from the vehicle battery, thereby inducing a braking force as the disc rotates in the magnetic field.

At the Willesden plant some 25 years design experience exists in this field of dynamometry. Attempts by the design staff some 10 years ago to get the Company to develop and simplify these eddycurrent dynamometers for mass production as retarders failed. It is felt, however, that the time is now opportune to reconsider this whole project.

In Britain public attention has been dramatically focused on the weaknesses of existing braking systems by the Yorkshire Coach disaster which claimed 32 lives in May 1975. The Sunday Times (1/6/75) states "last week's crash might have been avoided if the coach had been equipped with an extra braking device, such as an electromagnetic retarder which is being fitted to an increasing number of coaches in this country." In fact it would appear that only 10% of Britain's 75,000 buses and coaches actually have retarders fitted to them. There is, therefore, clearly a vast market available to Lucas if it adopts an imaginative approach to this problem. It is not suggested that Lucas should simply produce dynamometers; rather what is proposed is that they should analyze the whole nature of braking systems through a wide range of vehicles, including buses, coaches, articulated lorries, underground and overhead trains as used by British Rail.

It is proposed that a braking system analysis and development team should be set up to take an overview of this problem. The team should make an analysis of the actual requirements for the different applications, and at the same time should analyze any patent problems which might arise with respect of the French Labinal retarder which is marketed in this country as "Telma." Simultaneously a development team should develop an existing Lucas Aerospace dynamometer, using a unit capable of being fitted in the conventional position, i.e., in the prop shaft between the engine and the back axle, capable of absorbing 600 brake horse power and weighing approximately 200 kgs. Once this unit has been designed and developed, discussions should take place with Girlings to arrange for its mass production, i.e., under a licensing arrangement from Lucas Aerospace. Although a vast

potential market exists for dynamometers of this kind, this
unit should be seen only as the first step in evolving a
total braking system capability.

The second stage would be a combined electromagnetic
braking system coupled directly to a traditional mechanical
brake based on a Girling disc. The control system would have
to be designed such that by moving the brake pedal the dynamometer would initially operate and the further depression
of the pedal will gradually increase the current and hence
the braking load until finally the mechanical brake could be
applied if necessary. Use of the dynameter between the prop
shaft and the back axle clearly limits its range of application. To overcome this, discussion should take place with
manufacturers of gear boxes to arrange to have them fitted
on the output side of the gearbox such that they could be
used on the tractors of articulated vehicles.

A further development would be to design and produce
units which could be fitted to each individual axle. Work in
this field is already being carried out in France, but based
on traditional dynameter units.

An elaborate control system would be necessary to ensure
that as each of the individual axles is braked it still meets
the new EEC requirements concerning the sequence and the
effects on individual axles and their proper synchronization
to remove the risk of unstable skidding or "jack knifing."
This work would dovetail conveniently with existing work being undertaken by Girlings on anti-skid systems. It is important that this programme should not be carried out in the
usual piece-meal short-term manner. A long-term overall plan
should be worked out, and each stage of the development programme should be a tactical step towards a long-term strategy.

Part of that long-term strategy should be the provision
of radar applied braking systems. All the necessary components should be designed to produce a flexible range of system
options. Dynamometers lend themselves ideally to this as the
load is applied electrically. The 1975 Society of Automotive
Engineers Congress held in Detroit, reported that the National
Highway Safety Association's 71 statistics showed that 8% of
the vehicles on the road were involved in rear end accidents.
They represented 25% of accidents or 8-1/2 million vehicles.
The medium to long-term aim should be to provide radar applied braking systems particularly for use on motorways.

The <u>Financial Times</u> (7/5/75) stated:

In the longer run electronic station keeping
devices which use a form of radar to apply brakes

automatically to cars travelling along motorways
when they approach too close to a slowly moving
vehicle ahead may be adopted. If they were introduced compulsorily for traffic they would
certainly lead to a substantial reduction in the
number of lives lost through motorway accidents
in fog.

R. A. Chandler and L. E. Woods of the U.S. Department of
Commerce Institute for Telecommunication Sciences have said
at the conference quoted above "while significant problems
exist in the development of generally acceptable radar sen-
sors for automobile braking, no insurmountable difficulties
are evident." Applications more complex than mere station
keeping should also be considered, but these give rise to a
series of technological problems which, although they could
be overcome, may only be soluble with very expensive equipment. However both Chandler and Woods had the following to
say, "Both pedestrians and the cyclists are detectable, radiation hazards are minimal, small radius corners give a problem
in false alarm, inter-system blinding is a problem and that
the effect of rain scattering are serious." Spokesmen for
the National Highway Traffic Safety Association have stated
that research in radar braking fields warrants continuation,
but the decision to implement such devices should be made
only after cost-benefit studies and acceptable hardware
performance had been verified. It is clear that now is
the stage for Lucas to become involved in these developments.

It is proposed that a similar long-term overview should
be taken of braking requirements for rolling stock railways
and underground. Already British Rail has introduced, on an
experimental basis, velocity monitoring systems, which indicate to the driver if he is travelling at a velocity considered to be dangerous for an oncoming curve, junction or
other impediment. With these velocity sensing devices already installed, it would be a logical step to use this information to feed into braking systems such that the train
was automatically slowed down to meet the travelling requirements already determined for other sections of the track if
the driver fails to respond due to illness or whatever. Such
overall braking systems would require many computers and mi-
cro processors. The use of these would fit in with suggestions made elsewhere in the Corporate Plan.

Hybrid power pack. A somewhat more complicated device
is a new prime mover for vehicles. A lot of attention has
been focused recently on the possibility of using electronically propelled cars in cities; this would enormously reduce
pollution and of course gasoline consumption. However, the

problem is that on a stop/start journey the batteries have to
be recharged every 40 miles and on a flat continuous journey,
about every hundred miles. We are proposing a packaged prime
mover which makes the best use of the characteristics of an
internal combustion engine and an electric motor. Motor cars
commonly have to have an internal combustion engine about
three times the size that is actually required, simply in
order to overcome inertia. Moreover, a great deal of fuel
is wasted and a great deal of pollution produced during the
significant periods of idling, accelerating, stopping and
starting, etc. Our idea is basically of a small gasoline
engine, which would run continuously at its constant optimum
speed, which would drive a generator to continuously charge
one or two batteries and the batteries would in turn drive
either a single motor or 4 hub motors to propel the vehicle.
Our initial calculations show that you could reduce toxic
emissions by about 80%. The vehicle could also be very si-
lent as it would be running at a predetermined and constant
speed and therefore could be an effective silencing system on
the internal combustion engine.

Road/rail vehicle. The braking system and hybrid power
pack could of course be sold in its own right, and we suggest
that this should be done, but we also believe that both of
them should be incorporated into a quite revolutionary road/
rail vehicle that we are proposing. This would basically be
a light vehicle running on pneumatic tires and capable of
travelling through cities on normal roads, and then driving
directly onto normal rail tracks. We have already produced
a prototype of this vehicle which was shown on the BBC TV
programme "Tomorrows's World." We are currently attempting
to see whether that system would be of use in Third World
countries. The beauty of the system is that the best characteristics of trains could be allied to the best characteristics of road vehicles. For instance, a road/rail vehicle
running on concrete tracks could go up inclines of 1 in 6 or
7, instead of the usual 1 in 80 for railways - this cuts
civil engineering costs down dramatically which currently
run to about 1 million per railway track mile. Also, in
Third World countries it would be possible to modify existing
road vehicles to run on this sort of "railway" system. This
would obviously avoid the need for Third World countries
having to buy very expensive locomotives and rolling stock.
We are hopeful that we will be able to produce this idea in
Tanzania, and the Overseas Development Ministry of this
country is currently considering the project.

Other Proposals. In addition to those few product proposals just briefly described, the Corporate Plan proposes as
alternative socially useful products:

1. incontinence devices for geriatric patients
2. portable defibrillator for heart attack victims
3. kidney machine designs for dialysis in non-hospital settings
4. "hobcart" device to aid mobility for children suffering from Spina Bifida
5. research proposals in fuel cell technology
6. control systems for wind generators
7. gas-fired heat pump for cheap space heating
8. semi-robotic devices for oil pipeline inspection and repair
9. interactive work systems with numerical-control machine tools
10. skill-maintaining remote mining and firefighting equipment

How Has the Corporate Plan Fared?

The Combine presented a short introduction to their alternative corporate plan to the management of the company in January 1976 and they launched it publicly at the same time. They only presented the management with a short introduction, as they might otherwise have given away the equivalent of £five to ten million worth of technical consultancy done on their own time to a company which appeared to be more interested in making a profit than in maintaining jobs. This introduction basically laid out the steward's proposals for discussions and negotiations with the Company in the event of any further layoffs or closures.

Three months later the Company replied with a blank refusal to consider any of their proposals. The Company maintained that it was management's job to manage and workers' to work (unless of course it was to leave). They also could not accept the idea of socially useful products, maintaining that making military aerospace hardware was socially useful as it protected the "free world." The main reason for the plan's rejection, however, appeared to be the idea that it challenged management prerogative. The Company maintained that their employees' best employment interests would be served by going along with the company's own proposal. Almost exactly two years later, another 2000 layoffs were announced.

The Combine then approached the Trades Union Congress (TUC) and the Department of Industry to see if they could get some pressure and some sort of assistance from their own trade union leadership and from a Labour Government. The TUC was however unable to deal with the matter as the relevant employer's representative refused to consider anything of

this sort. The Department of Industry meanwhile maintained
that they could not intervene, until and unless there had
been some progress made in the Company, and apparently the
Department of Industry at that time seemed to feel that the
Company management was in fact discussing and negotiating
with the Combine Committee on this matter.

1977 heralded layoffs. In February, Lucas Aerospace
announced that they had a "labour surplus" of 1,100. An
overtime ban and selective boycotting of the movement of
parts was enforced, and the Combine threatened further industrial action if the layoffs were implemented. The layoff
threat collapsed in the face of this industrial action, which
itself was supported by some quite considerable political
support from outside Lucas Aerospace, support which came from
people backing the alternative corporate plan.

The Transport and General Workers Union, the largest
trade union in Britain, at their 1977 delegate conference
expressed clear support for the struggle by the Combine. A
document entitled "Military Spending, Defence Cuts and Alternative Employment" which was produced by the General Executive Council was passed by the Conference. This document
called on workers to pursue alternative corporate plans, and
it called on the Government to institute planning agreements
with companies wherever and whenever this sort of shop steward initiative arose. Many of the Combine were at that time
advocating a planning agreement procedure in Lucas Aerospace;
they maintained that the Company was receiving very large
amounts of taxpayers' money through the Industry Acts, and
through tax deferrals and stock appreciation (in reality tax
concessions to companies to help them through inflation).

Towards the end of 1977 the Combine started to notice
management rumors about over capacity and too many people in
Lucas Aerospace. Meanwhile the Department of Industry had
changed its tune somewhat and now maintained that the Combine
Committee must proceed through so-called official union channels. The Combine Committee had in fact been recognized for
certain purpose by the Company before it launched its corporate plan, but was no longer regarded as a negotiating body
by the Company thereafter. In the ensuing years the Company
has made a number of moves toward recognizing the Combine
Committee. (Also in 1978 the Combine Committee developed the
Centre for Alternative Industrial and Technological Systems
(CAITS), a technical research and support organization based
at the North East London Polytechnic, run jointly by the
Polytechnic and the Combine Shop Stewards Committee.) As
mentioned earlier, in March 1978, almost exactly two years
after the Company had originally rejected the Plan a further

2000 layoffs were announced, with factory closures at Liverpool, Bradford, Shipley, and Coventry. The Combine tried to
get the Department of Industry to put pressure on the Company
not to carry out these plans. There were a number of meetings with members of Parliament and others during April and
May, and in June the Department of Industry announced an
£8 million subsidy package for Lucas Aerospace, which was
supposed to maintain 500 of the 2,000 jobs threatened. This
£8 million involved £6 million to build a specialized factory
in Huyton and £2 million to build a new factory in Bradford,
both with substantial rent free periods, and with grants for
assistance with new equipment (much of which has subsequently
been seen to be labour-saving).

Combine members managed to obtain some paid time off
work for a group of 14 stewards to draw up alternative proposals in place of factory closures threatened by Lucas.
This committee, the Lucas Aerospace Confederation Trade Union
Committee, was convened under the aegis of the Confederation
of Shipbuilding and Engineering Unions (CSEU). It was allowed two months in which to visit each site, put questions to
the management and draw up a negotiating document for purposes for saving all 2,000 jobs. At the 1978 Annual Conference of the Labour Party there was unanimous support for a
resolution supporting the Lucas workers and calling for the
implementation of a planning agreement procedure on the basis
of their alternative corporate plan.

Towards the end of 1978 the working party of shop stewards produced a report entitled "Lucas Aerospace - Turning
Industrial Decline Into Expansion - A Trade Union Initiative," and this report specified a number of products, their
labour requirements, government assistance and so on which
would be needed to maintain all of those jobs currently
threatened, and in the places where they already exist, i.e.,
in Liverpool, Bradford and Coventry. This report drew heavily on the alternative corporate plan, but was made quite
specific to the sites and labour forces threatened from
March 1978. This report was a subject of negotiations with
the Department of Industry and the Company in February 1979,
the formal result of that meeting was the maintenance of the
£8 million offer to Lucas, but this time 800 jobs were to be
saved instead of just 500. The Combine rejected this agreement, but were hampered by the fact that there had been official union support of the deal. Nevertheless, in March 1979
a CSEU delegate conference also condemned the agreement.

Since then the Combine Committee has managed to maintain almost all of those jobs threatened, except for the
closure of a small foundry in Coventry (about 30 people), and

a small amount of redundancies in Bradford. In all, the Company has managed to lay off only about 50 of the 2,000 called for in its original plan.

Despite the fact that the Combine Committee is still having to fight hard to get the Company to take the product proposals seriously, the mobilization and the challenges made to the Company's policies have in fact enabled the Combine to drastically reduce the rate of redundancies in the Company. Almost alone, in the massive cutbacks in British manufacturing jobs, this Combine has been able to stem the tide. The Corporate Plan has provided a rallying point and a powerful challenge to corporate policies which always seem to place the burden of its restructuring and reorganization on the shoulders of the workforce.

Right up to the present, the Combine Committee continues to pursue policies in line with its alternative corporate plan, although a number of new plans and new documents and new bargaining positions have been developed over the years in response to, and often in advance of problems in particular sites or areas of business. The Combine seems to have managed to develop its information gathering system to quite a sophisticated level, which helps it to not only respond to management attacks as effectively as possible, but also to deal with threats in advance.

The idea of socially useful work has continued to be a major theme of the Combine's activities. It has led them into alliances with groups of workers from other industries, from the National Health Service and elsewhere. Other combine committees have been formed at a number of firms in the U.K. The Lucas Aerospace Combine Shop Stewards Committee has tried to seize the initiative and demonstrate in the most concrete and pragmatic way that it is neither necessary nor desirable for considerations of the maintenance of work in military industry firms to lead employees into dependence and hence support of ever escalating military budgets. We have tried to chart a constructive path to highlight not only the existence of alternatives to dependence on military-oriented production, but also the enormous social benefit achievable by redirecting the skills and talents of the military industrial labour force toward such socially useful production.

References

1. *Economist* (May 3, 1975), p. 113.

2. *New Scientist* (March 21, 1974), p. 732.

3. Sheridan, G., *The Guardian* (June 27, 1974).

4. Civeyrel, F., *Vision* (February 1975), p. 41.

5. "NEDC Report on Process Plant," *Financial Times* (June 10, 1975), p. 9.

6. Ibid.

7. "Subsea Technology," *Financial Times* (April 23, 1975), p. 2.

8. Ibid.

9. Op. cit., Civeyrel, F.

10. Rosenbrock, H., "Future of Control," UMIST Report (August 1975).

8. The Political Economy of Reversing the Arms Race

Economic Conversion as a Strategy for Social Change

    The term "economic conversion" has been used here to refer to the transfer of labor, capital and other productive resources from unproductive military use to alternative civilian-oriented activity. The problem, of course, is to assure that this transfer of resources takes place as smoothly as possible, with minimal economic and social disruption. And we have seen that it _is_ a problem, despite the enormous economic and social benefits that would potentially flow from such a transfer. For once resources have been occupied in one particular use for a significant period of time, there is a tendency for them to become less flexible, more specialized. This economic stiffening of the joints can generally be overcome without great difficulty if approached properly, particularly in the case of labor. But it will not happen automatically. Careful attention is required for the conversion process to be smooth and effective.

    It is true that economic conversion, so defined, is but a special case of the broader problem of "economic transition," the transfer of productive resources among any specified set of alternative uses (a vastly understudied problem made vital by the inherently dynamic nature of economies). Yet, it is a particularly important special case because of the economically parasitic effects of the production of military goods and services, not to mention the devastating effects of their use, made ever more likely by their continued development and accumulation. There is no other transfer of resources that stands as such a crucial prerequisite to both economic viability and physical survival.[1]

    But why discuss conversion now? Isn't it a little like locking the barn door before the horse is purchased? There are no plans for reducing the military budget, much less for

even partial disarmament. Quite the contrary, the Carter
Administration, which carried out year-by-year expansions in
the military budget above the rate of inflation, has been
replaced by the Reagan Administration which is even more
militaristic and appears deeply committed to a far larger and
more dangerous escalation of the arms race. The Cold War,
restarted by the Carter Administration is being pursued with
such vigor and enthusiasm by President Reagan that confronta-
tion and "hot war" seem even more likely. Another Vietnam
War lies waiting in the wings in Latin America and/or Africa,
with apparently significant public support. The vested
interests that support the continuation of the present extraordinarily high levels of military spending are no less
powerful, and in fact seem to have not only seized the initiative, but also many of the critical seats of power. What
is the point of talking about conversion now?

Changes in the status quo that go against the "conventional wisdom" are virtually always viewed as threats by the
mainstream of society, regardless of how beneficial they may
be. And any world view that faces off against the conventional wisdom no matter how logical, no matter how rooted in
reality, must always contend not only with societal inertia
but also with the outright hostility which inevitably arises
from being perceived as a threat. It is therefore necessary,
if one is to be effective in advocating social directional
changes of this type, to find a strategy for removing enough
of this threat perception to permit people to allow themselves to listen to what is being said. Belief in the moral
and intellectual persuasiveness of the argument being advo-
cated should never be allowed to blind one to the necessity
of reducing threat perception. It is simply not possible, no
matter how obvious the case being argued, to persuade anyone
who is not listening.

Economic conversion is a strategy for making peace
possible by concretely reassuring those who directly fear
loss of their own jobs as a result of cutbacks in military
spending, as well as the much larger segment of the population who fear that such cutbacks will generate unemployment
(or broader economic recession or depression.)

As has been argued in the preceding chapters, persistently high levels of military spending have been and continue to be enormously damaging to the economies of both the
U.S. and the U.S.S.R. The idea that high military expenditures are detrimental to any economy may not yet have pene-
trated the consciousness of the wider public. But it is
nevertheless true. Hence, economic conversion can be understood as a crucial positive policy for economic redevelopment
and reconstruction. Seen in that light, it is not only not

threatening, nor merely reassuring, but a positively attractive and encouraging approach.

Furthermore, the previous chapters have shown that the economic conversion problem, though it is certainly a complex one, is without question solvable, whether in the context of a fundamentally socialist or market capitalist oriented economic system. It is possible, given careful advanced planning, to convert resources currently involved in military activity to productive civilian use--not merely to create the same total number of new civilian jobs as the number of military jobs lost, but to create the kind of civilian jobs which will productively absorb those specific people released from military activity, and to assure a smooth transition between the two. One possible model for institutionalizing the process of advance contingency planning for conversion, embodied in the proposed Defense Economic Adjustment Act, has been described and discussed. And the origins, nature and history of one set of alternative product plans, the Lucas stewards "Corporate Plan" has also been set forth. It should be clear then that economic conversion is not merely a nice idea, but a hardnosed, down-to-earth policy.

Of course, the current consensus in support of large military budgets in the U.S. is not based solely on the belief that military spending is economically beneficial and/ or that the transition to lower levels of military spending would in itself be unacceptably disruptive. There are also serious questions of military national security involved.[2] Yet the political power of the perceived economic threat of reduced military spending is not to be underestimated. It is, in fact, clearly understood by the military and military industry. Even a cursory glance at press accounts of the pro- and anti-B1 bomber campaigns, for example, will reveal that the debate centered, not on the strategic value of the B1, but on the economic effects (particularly the job issue). The political importance of the job argument can also be verified by noting that virtually every newspaper account of any curtailment of military activity, whether a base closure or contract cancellation, always contains a statement about job loss, if not in the headline, then in the first sentence.

Just how much of the support for large military budgets would evaporate if planning for conversion rendered the jobs argument irrelevant is difficult to say. But one thing is absolutely clear. The debate on weapons systems, military posture, etc. would be moved from the arena of myopic economics into the areas of appropriate political behavior and legitimate military requirements where it belongs. The military is no social economic welfare agency, nor should it be. National security issues should not be unnecessarily entangled in local economic dependencies. No military project need ever, or should ever, be funded for economic reasons. There are always more effective and more generally productive ways of creating or maintaining jobs and income in a local community than by building unnecessary military hardware or keeping an unneeded base open.

The Opening Door

Actually this is an important time to be pressing forward on the conversion front. A variety of new potential constituencies for a shifting of economic priorities are opening up as a consequence of our deepening economic malaise. And conversion planning is being increasingly perceived by some as the way to bring about the shifting of priorities without threatening jobs or creating significant personal economic disruption.

A key development of the past few years has been the growing interest and involvement of labor unions in the U.S. in the conversion issue. One of the nation's two largest trade unions representing workers in military industry, the International Association of Machinists and Aerospace Workers (IAM) under the leadership of William Winpisinger has put itself solidly behind the concept of conversion. In Chapter Five, IAM President Winpisinger presented a clear statement of the union's commitment to operationalizing a broad economic reconstruction strategy of which economic conversion is a key component. In May 1981, the IAM began taking concrete steps in this direction by beginning to forge a working connection between the academic community involved in this set of issues and local representatives of the union at a meeting held in New York. The other such union, the United Automobile, Aerospace and Agricultural Implement Workers Union (UAW) under the leadership of Douglas Fraser, has participated along with a series of major U.S. unions including the United Electrical, Radio and Machine Workers of America (UE), the American Federation of Government Employees (AFGE), and the Oil, Chemical and Atomic Workers Union (OCAW), among others, in serious discussions relative to the conversion question over the past several years.

Why have the unions become involved in the conversion issue? The chief motivation appears to be a deep concern with the persistence of high levels of unemployment, combined with a growing awareness that military spending is at best a poor way of creating jobs and at worst a direct source of unemployment. It has begun to be understood that while new military projects create jobs with one hand, they destroy far more jobs with the other by undermining the competitiveness of domestic civilian industry through the pre-emption of

crucial economic resources. For unions, the diminishing
competitive ability of U.S. industry, which has often been
laid on their backs, is very much a bread and butter issue--
a constant threat to their ability to achieve higher wages,
and even more important, to the job security of their members.
They are becoming more aware that a transfer of resources
from the military to the civilian sector is the only way
domestic industry can be made more competitive without a
major rollback of the wage rates, fringe benefits and working
condition improvements they have fought so long and hard to
obtain. Even so, the emerging support is strongly conditioned on careful conversion planning to assure a smooth
transition process and the continued employment of those
fellow unionists who work in the military sector.

Local Governments

State and local government officials constitute another
potential constituency for conversion, though one which at
present is far more tentative than that of the unions.
Caught in a tightening squeeze between the rising cost of
providing basic government services, much of which is induced
or at least exacerbated by high rates of inflation,[3] and
growing public resistance to tax increases, they confront
financial problems ranging from the unpleasant to the
catastrophic. In its more extreme manifestations, as at the
height of the New York City financial crisis, local decision
power has been usurped by outside emergency financial control boards, established as part of the price for rescue
efforts--never a pleasant prospect for decision makers.
State and local officials find themselves increasingly in a
no win situation, forced to choose between increasing taxes
or layoffs of teachers, firefighters, police, sanitation
workers, etc. They face longer and more frequent strikes by
public employees fighting to at least slow the rate at which
their wages are being cut by inflation and their work loads
are being increased by understaffing due to hiring freezes or
worse.[4]

The money they need is, of course, there--in most cases,
within the communities themselves. But year by year it flows
toward Washington in an avalanche of tax dollars the largest
fraction of which is spent in the unproductive military
sector. Conversion offers an economically and socially
responsible way to tap into the roughly $2350 the average
U.S. household was, for example, paying for military goods
and services in fiscal year 1979.

Paradoxically, in regions where military spending is the
heaviest (and it is very unevenly distributed geographically),
state and local governments have the strongest vested interest

in at least planning for conversion. Such areas cannot help
but be aware of both the fickleness of particular military
spending projects and the growing technological displacement
of workers in military industry. Even when the military
budget is expanding, some contracts are terminated and some
bases are closed. The Pentagon, for instance, announced
plans for cuts at another 107 military bases in April 1978
in the face of a record military budget.[5] The closure of a
military base or cancellation of a major military contract
can create economic disaster in a given community, unless
plans for conversion of the facilities to civilian use are
developed. A Department of Defense report of the job effects
of 22 base closures around the U.S. show a _gain_ of nearly
27,000 jobs after conversion (though years were required for
the recovery because there had been no advance planning).[6]

At minimum, then, planning for conversion constitutes
an economic insurance policy for defense dependent communities. Actual implementation of conversion plans could
provide even more economic security for those communities
through a diversification of their economic base.

What evidence is there that the door to this constituency may be gradually opening? On June 18, 1978 at the U.S.
Conference of Mayors in Atlanta, "Mayor after mayor took the
microphone...to demand, in a departure from tradition, that
the Federal Government spend less rather than more."[7] This
was obviously in reaction to the fear of widespread taxpayer
revolt generated by the passage of Proposition 13 in California earlier that month. Clearly the mayors had in mind a
reduction of the Federal tax bite so that more of whatever
tax potential did exist would be available to them. But, as
was pointed out to them, Federal spending for aid to local
governments has increased from $7 billion to $80 billion in
less than two decades. Since it obviously makes no sense for
them to press for Federal cuts here, they will have to look
elsewhere. And it will be very difficult for them to continue to do so without noticing the whopping $162 billion
military budget.

Furthermore, in the past few years an increasing number
of discussions on the economic impacts of military spending
and the process of conversion have been attended or participated in by city council people, directors of state and city
chambers of commerce, various county government officials and
at least one big city mayor. There have not been a great
many people involved, but they have included officials from
some of the nation's most heavily defense dependent areas.
The arguments have not necessarily been welcomed with open
arms, but neither have they been summarily dismissed. The
point is that there is serious discussion and it is growing.

The Tax Revolt

The tax revolters themselves also constitute a strong potential constituency for conversion. In 1978, California's Proposition 13 aimed at slashing property taxes by 57%, but even a brief analysis of the anatomy of the individual fiscal tax burden will show that the taxpayer revolt was focused on one of its minor components. To date, none of the spokespersons for this movement have come to grips with the fact that the "Military tax" by itself constitutes a clearly larger part of the total burden than does the property tax. All the data that follow are standardized for 1977, unless otherwise noted.[8] They are only intended to represent relative magnitudes.

The tax burden borne by individuals has three major components: income taxes, sales taxes and property taxes. Both income and sales taxes are paid to federal as well as state and local governments, but the property tax is the province of state and local government alone. Individual income taxes are predominantly federal, with 84% of collection, as against 16% at state and local levels. Gross receipts and sales taxes, on the other hand, are mostly state and local with 75%, as against 28% federal (the latter includes customs duties). As a national average, the relative sizes of these three main components of the individual tax burden were as follows: property taxes, the target of the California-based tax revolters, constituted only 19%; sales taxes accounted for 25%; and income taxes were responsible for 56%. Nearly half the total weight of these individual taxes, some 47%, was taken in the form of _federal_ income tax dollars.

The average U.S. taxpayer thus paid roughly $2.50 in federal income tax for every dollar of property tax. These individual income tax dollars constituted 64% of the total tax revenue collected by the federal government.

And how were the federal revenues spent? The largest part of the federal budget outlays, 73% in 1977 (up to 75% in 1979) were classified as "relatively uncontrollable" by the U.S. Office of Management and Budget (OMB). Deleting "Prior-year contracts and obligations" from this category to leave only "open-ended programs and fixed costs" such as social security, unemployment insurance, federal employee retirement, veteran benefits, Medicare and Medicaid, etc. bring the percentage down to 59% in that year (58% in 1979). OMB classifies these as "relatively uncontrollable" because they "...can neither be increased nor decreased by presidential decisions without a change in existing federal laws or are beyond administrative control, such as benefit payments that beneficiaries are entitled to by law..."[9]

On the other hand, "relatively controllable" outlays are those whose magnitudes are essentially decided upon year-by-year. In 1977, a total of $112.9 billion of federal expenditures were so classified by the OMB ($128.6 billion in 1979). Of these $70.8 billion ($71.7 billion in 1979) were put by OMB in the category of "national defense" expenditures. Thus, adhering precisely to OMB definition, 63% (56% in 1979) of controllable federal outlays were for military-related purposes. If "prior-year" contracts are added on the theory that they were at least partly the result of "controllable" outlays of past years, the percentage which OMB classified as national defense expenditures becomes 53% (49% in 1979.)

Since the system of budgeting and administrative categories is complex, and all systems of accounting categories are essentially arbitrary, it is possible to manipulate the evaluation of federal expenditure in so many ways that the process of budget analysis can become very confusing. In addition, whole sections of functionally important expenditures often appear under classifications quite different from what would normally be expected by those not initiated into the mysteries of the federal budget. For example, one would certainly expect that expenditures for the development and production of nuclear weapons would be included in the budget for the Department of Defense. However, they are instead located in the budget of the Department of Energy.

Trying to disentangle the situation sufficiently to accurately estimate the fraction of the individual's tax burden that supports military spending is, for these and other reasons, no mean task. Only the roughest sort of estimate is attempted here.

Certain funds are "dedicated" to specific purposes through the establishment of separately financed trust funds. For instance, the social security system is financed by separate payroll taxes on covered employees and their employers. These funds cannot legally be spent for any other purpose (which is why they are classified as "relatively uncontrollable") and so can be functionally segregated from general income tax flows. Those taxes categorized as "individual income" taxes are not used to support these specially funded programs. If the major categories of separately financed funds[10] are eliminated from the calculation, remaining federal expenditures total $282.6 billion in 1977 ($358.4 billion in 1979). Of this, some $124.7 billion ($150 billion in 1979) or 44% (42% in 1979) is clearly military related.[11]

It is reasonable to consider this a conservative estimate of the general tax financed budget share of military

spending.[12] If this is counterposed against the estimate
resulting from considering only "controllable outlays" a
range of 44% - 63% can be derived for 1977. Assuming that
individual income taxes were spent in these relative propor-
tions for military purposes, the direct "military tax"
burden of individuals is at least 10%, and perhaps as much as
58% greater than their property tax burden.

The overall picture may be summarized as follows. The
property taxes, which were the subject of the tax revolt,
constitute only about one-fifth of the average individual's
direct tax burden. These taxes went to state and local
governments, primarily to finance local services such as
education, police and fire services, and sanitation, as well
as public welfare. Federal income taxes, on the other hand,
are responsible for nearly half the individual's direct tax
burden. Almost two-thirds of "controllable" federal outlays
went for military purposes. In 1977, the average U.S.
citizen paid $2.50 in federal income tax for every dollar
paid in state and local property tax. The part of the individual's tax burden taken as "military tax" can be roughly
estimated as somewhere between $1.10 and $1.60 per dollar of
property tax.

Furthermore, spending on the military involves double
taxation; the first tax involves the taxpayer loss of purchasing power as dollars taken in income tax to be used for
military purposes; the second tax involves the loss of purchasing power as the inflation, which the military spending
has played a primary role in generating, robs those dollars
that remain part of their value. Therefore, even if only an
appropriate fraction of any cut in military spending were
directly returned to the taxpayers, they would receive more
tax relief, dollar for dollar, than if other forms of governmental spending were cut. And the fraction not returned
could be shifted to the increased provision of various vital
government services as education, police and fire protection,
urban reconstruction, etc.

It is, of course, not only those who have actively
engaged in one form or another of the tax revolt, but the
broader middle class plagued by rising taxes and continuing
inflation, battling ever harder to maintain a standard of
living they have been taught to expect, to whom a door may
slowly be opening.

Business and Banking

Important components of the business and banking community may also come to support the concept of conversion. The

falling value of the dollar and the attendant instability of
the international monetary system may leave room for profitable currency speculation, but in the longer term instability
is nearly always bad for business. Instability means uncertainty and uncertainty can be dangerous. Much of the
dollar's troubles have been publicly laid to the rising price
of and dependency on imported oil. It is interesting to note
that as of the first five months of 1978 the dollar outflow
due to oil imports (15.9 billion) was smaller than that due
to either imports of machinery and transport equipment
($19.1 billion) or manufactured goods ($18.2 billion).[13] It
is the military sector induced failing competitiveness of
U.S. industry and not simply the price of oil which is crippling the dollar as an international currency.

While it is true that business, especially big business,
has far greater mobility to run away from its problems and
far greater flexibility to protect itself by financial
diversification than do workers or communities, it does not
follow that business enjoys watching important segments of
its market evaporate. Even U.S. based multinationals may be
leery of the revival of protectionist sentiment which has,
as was inevitable, accompanied the growing invasion of
imports.

It is, in fact, true that a smooth transfer of resources
from the military to the civilian sector would be good for
business. And what is good for business will not indefi-
nitely escape the attention of at least the more open-minded
and forward-looking business people and bankers.

During the past few years, in a very small scale and
tentative way, the conversion question has begun to be
raised here. It is far too soon even to speculate on how
this will proceed.

Organized Religion

For many years such religious groups as the Mennonites
and segments of the Quakers have been deeply and actively
involved in pressing forward on anti-militarist, peace
issues. But more and more religious organizations, some of
a much more conservative bent, have begun to take up the
issue of the reversal of the arms race. For example, the
annual convention of the Southern Baptists, meeting in
Atlanta in June 1978, unanimously passed a resolution
calling for a transference of funds from "nuclear weapons to
basic human needs." The New York Times report of that
latter event noted "The gesture was the latest in a series
of signs that the disarmament issue is stirring religious

leaders in evangelical circles as well as in the Roman
Catholic Church and liberal Protestant demoninations."[14]

In an interview in <u>Sojourners</u> magazine in 1979, one of
the best known evangelical Christian leaders in the U.S.,
former confidant to Presidents, Billy Graham said,

> "The present arms race is a terrifying
> thing, and it is almost impossible to
> overestimate its potential for disaster.
> <u>...Is a nuclear holocaust inevitable</u>
> <u>if the arms race is not stopped?</u>
> <u>Frankly, the answer is almost certainly</u>
> <u>yes</u>. Now I know that some people feel
> human beings are so terrified of a
> nuclear war that no one would dare start
> one. I wish I could accept that. But
> neither history nor the Bible gives much
> reason for optimism....I honestly wish we
> had never developed nuclear weapons. I
> cannot see any way in which nuclear war
> could be branded as being God's will.
> Such warfare if it ever happens, will
> come because of the greed and pride and
> covetousness of the human heart...I am
> not a pacifist, but I fervently hope and
> pray our differences will never become
> an excuse for nuclear war....I wish we
> were working on Salt X right now! Total
> destruction of nuclear arms..." (emphasis
> added)

Even more recently, drawn into the arms race issue in a
very dramatic way by proposals to build the MX land-based
mobile missile system in Utah and Nevada, the Mormon Church
too has begun to join the forces opposing the arms race. In
a statement issued by the Mormon leadership on May 5, 1981,
the nuclear arms race was characterized as in direct conflict
with the core of the Church's purpose and teachings:

> "Our fathers came to this western area to
> establish a base from which to carry the
> gospel of peace to the peoples of the
> earth. It is ironic, and a denial of the
> very essence of that gospel, that in this
> same general area there should be con-
> structed a mammoth weapons system poten-
> tially capable of destroying much of
> civilization...
> "...history indicates that men have seldom

seldom created armaments that
eventually were not put to use."

Several years ago, shortly after becoming the chief
minister of the Riverside Church in New York City, Rev.
William Sloane Coffin set up the Riverside Disarmament Project, in an attempt to reach out to an interdenominational
congregation of religious organizations and stimulate their
interest and concern in working for the reversal of the arms
race. The Riverside Project has successfully catalyzed the
holding of a well-attended series of church-based confer-
ences on the arms race throughout the U.S. Some of these
have given rise to other ongoing activist anti-arms race
religious projects such as the Interfaith Center to Reverse
the Arms Race, formed and operated jointly by the Episcopal
All Saints Church in Pasadena, California, and the Jewish
Leo Beck Temple in Los Angeles. And, of course, the spiri-
tual leader of the world's millions of Roman Catholics, Pope
John Paul II has repeatedly and eloquently pointed to the
crying need for a reduction in world militarism.

More and more, it has become clear to these church-
based peace activists that economic conversion stands as a
key piece in moving from the desire, the felt need to
reverse the arms race and the realization of that need. It
is important to understand that the opening of these various
doors in no way implies that the movement for economic conversion will inevitably be successful. But it does imply
opportunity, an opportunity that implies a directed path for
concrete, pragmatic social and political action.

Broadening the Constituency for Conversion

One of the most hopeful processes now clearly underway
is the growing awareness among key organizations, operating
in areas as apparently diverse as labor, peace, ecology,
economic development, religion, antipoverty, etc., of a
commonality of interests centering on the military issue.
There are three main rallying points. The first and most
basic is survival. We all have differing perspectives on
how much time is required to bring about the changes in the
human condition that we seek, but all agree that it will
take time. And the escalation of the nuclear arms race and
the reality of nuclear proliferation make it unclear how
much time we have left. As Nobel laureate biologist George
Wald reminded us so eloquently a decade ago, before it makes
sense to plan for the future, we must first be sure that we
have a future:

"There is nothing worth having that can be

obtained by nuclear war: nothing
material or ideological, no tradition that it can defend. It is
utterly self defeating... Nuclear
weapons offer us nothing but a
balance of terror; and a balance
of terror is still terror.
"We have to get rid of those atomic
weapons, here and everywhere. We
cannot live with them...

"... Unless we can be surer than we
now are that this generation has a
future, nothing else matters. It's
not good enough to give it tender,
loving care, to supply it with break-
fast foods, to buy it expensive edu-
cations. Those things don't mean
anything unless this generation has
a future. And we're not sure that it
does."[6]

It is becoming increasingly clear that the present path
of the arms race is nonviable, and that if it continues we
will have the dubious honor of being the first species on
this planet responsible for its own extinction.

The second rallying point is the severe constraint put on
the availability of public revenues for any of a variety of socially useful purposes by the absorption of half the discretionary
Federal budget by the military. And the third is the critical potential contribution of the labor and other productive
resources now in the military sector to the revitalization
of the U.S. economy in general, as well as to specific goals
like development of alternate energy, reduction of environmental pollution, improvement of health care, Third World
economic development, etc. While it is not true that the
mere transference of military sector resources to productive
uses will guarantee either economic prosperity or the solution of critical societal problems, it is increasingly clear
that failure to redirect these resources will cripple any
meaningful attempts to deal effectively with these problems.

Evidence of the increasing tendency to see the inter-
relatedness of organizational concerns, and the value of
defining and exploring paths for joint action and mutual
support can be found in a variety of recent local, national
and even international activities and events. For example,
the major April 1978 demonstration for the closure of the
nuclear weapons plant at Rocky Flats, Colorado (near Denver),
and the conversion of its resources to productive civilian

use was very much a joint peace/ecology activity, supported by groups such as Environmentalists for Full Employment, Environmental Action of Colorado, the Clamshell Alliance, etc. as well as SANE, the Fellowship of Reconciliation, Women's Strike for Peace, and so on. Interestingly enough, the religious-linked organizations involved included not only the American Friends Service Committee and Clergy and Laity Concerned, but also the Archdiocesan Peace and Justice Office (Denver), the Board of Church and Society of the United Methodist Church, and the Jewish Peace Fellowship among others.

The massive demonstration for reversal of the arms race held at Dag Hammarskjold Plaza in New York in late May 1978 included about 10,000–15,000 demonstrators of an impressive variety of ages, ethnic backgrounds and organizational affiliations, including women's groups, the Grey Panthers, black, chicano and native American groups, labor unions, religious organizations of a number of faiths, ecologists and peace organizations. More formally, the United Nations Special Session on Disarmament, taking place across the street from this demonstration, resulted in the adoption of a proposal by the Nordic countries for a special UN study on the interrelationship between disarmament and development (a proposal that strongly emphasized the importance of economic conversion, and resulted in support of the research project underlying Chapter Three).

On a more local level, organizations like the Mid-Peninsula Conversion Project (MPCP) (located in the heart of a dense concentration of military industry in California, the nation's largest defense contracting state), are trying to work with government, labor, community, religious and other social action groups to foster awareness of mutual concern and joint action. The MPCP, one of the best developed and effective of these groups, has among other things been involved in developing a study of the potential for conversion from military activity to ecologically rational solar energy activity in California, and beyond. The Trident Conversion Campaign (Connecticut), the Texecon (Texas), the St. Louis Economic Conversion Project (Missouri), Live Without Trident (Washington), the Economic Conversion Project (New Mexico) and the Economic Conversion Project (Colorado) are other examples of locally focused organizations working in this vein. A number of national organizations like the American Friends Service Committee (AFSC), the Fellowship of Reconciliation (FOR) and SANE have additional local projects around the U.S. operating with a similar philosophy. For several years now AFSC and FOR have jointly sponsored the Nuclear Weapons Facilities Project to serve as liaison and facilitate communications between the various local organizing groups focusing their opposition around particular manufacturing, storage, etc. facilities that are the critical nodes of the nuclear arms race. These local groups are playing an absolutely critical role in reaching into the newly opening doors and generally raising consciousness at the grass roots level to the economic and security implications of the arms race.

There are also a number of organizations serving as information and expertise resource centers for these various groups as well as performing the separate but connected function of disseminating such information through other channels. Two of the most interesting and effective have been the Center for Defense Information in Washington, D.C. (directed by a retired rear admiral) and the Conversion Information Center of the Council on Economic Priorities in New York City.

There are, of course, many other organizations in the nation's capital and throughout the country each playing a role in this process of public education. Those mentioned above are merely meant to convey the flavor of the diversity, both geographical and in terms of approach, they represent. Yet virtually all of them have come, in recent years, to take the issue of economic conversion very seriously.

Other bits and pieces of evidence are found in such events as the explicit entry of the widely respected anti-nuclear power Union of Concerned Scientists into the arms race issue as a major part of their program and the formation of the Mobilization for Survival, a broad coalition of peace, ecology, religious, etc. groups.

It is important to understand that none of the variety of organizations slowly coming together on economic conversion are in any sense abandoning or even downgrading their fundamental organizational objectives. Rather they are becoming increasingly aware that they can move a considerable distance along the same path together while forwarding, not compromising their particular goals. This is a process of potentially spectacular significance.

However, lest we get carried away in a euphoric vision of the "forces of righteousness" moving side by side toward a humane world, it is necessary to realize that all of these diverse positive events, important though they may be, constitute only the beginning of a beginning. The reality is that the arms race is continuing, U.S. and world military spending is rising, and extremist right wing militaristic

groups like the American Security Council and the Committee
on the Present Danger are alive and well and in fact are
presently in key advice and control positions within the
Federal Government as the result of the sharp swing to the
right represented by the 1980 national election.

Conclusions

Economic conversion is a viable strategy for making
peace possible. It is very much a hard-nosed, pragmatic
approach. The plain fact is that the nation's economy will
never more than temporarily emerge from the deepening morass
of stagflation until it is relieved of the crippling burden
of heavy military spending. Furthermore, national security
will continue to deteriorate as long as we persist in the
fantasy that our safety can be assured by adding ever more
sophisticated weaponry to the nearly incomprehensible pile
of mutually destructive capability we have already amassed.
Yet until the fear of unemployment and other severe economic
disruption can be permanently laid to rest, it will be
exceedingly difficult to develop the political wherewithal
required to transfer resources from the military to the
civilian sector. And this is the crucial role of economic
conversion.

References

1. For one scenario of how a general nuclear war might even
    be generated wholly unintentionally, see Dumas, L. J.
    "Holocaust by Accident" in To Avoid Catastrophe, M. P.
    Hamilton, ed. (Eerdmans, Grand Rapids, 1977.)

2. For an analysis of the military/technical grounds for
    believing that the maintenance and expansion of military
    systems, apart from its economic effects, reduces nation-
    al security, see L. J. Dumas, "National Insecurity in
    the Nuclear Age," and "Human Fallibility and Weapons,"
    in The Bulletin of the Atomic Scientists (May 1976 and
    November 1980, respectively.)

3. See, for example, Edward Cowan, "Inflation Compounding
    Problems of State and City Governments," New York
    Times (June 7, 1978).

4. Even such basic city services as water supply and sewage
    are severely threatened in many major U.S. cities by
    decades of neglect of maintenance and repair because of
    financial difficulties--see John Herbers, "Beneath the
    Streets, Old Cities Crumble and Decay," New York

Times (April 9, 1978); see also Philip Shabecoff, "Safe
U.S. Drinking Water Is no Longer a Certainty," New York
Times (April 9, 1978).

5. "Pentagon Plans Cuts in 107 Military Bases," New
York Times (April 27, 1978).

6. Economic Recovery: Community Response to Defense
Decision to Close Bases, Defense Office of Economic
Adjustment (Washington, D.C., 1975).

7. Robert Reinhold, "Cuts in U.S. Spending Urged at Conference of Nation's Mayors," New York Times (June 19,
1978).

8. Bureau of the Census, U.S. Department of Commerce,
Statistical Abstract of the United States, 1979, pp. 256
and 287. The data given are not "pure". For example,
corporate income to localities is included with
"individual income," where it is apparently very small
relative to the pure category. It is beyond the scope
of this paper to sort out all the data impurities in
these tax figures. They are judged to be minor. In any
case, the percentages given for the distribution of the
tax burden are intended only to be indicative of the
relative share of different components. The analysis
presented is not overly sensitive to errors of the order
of magnitude these impurities are likely to represent.

9. Op. cit., Bureau of the Census, p. 256.

10. Social security and railroad retirement, federal employees retirement and insurance, and unemployment
assistance are included here.

11. Included in military related expenditures here are
present-year defense spending, prior-year defense contracts and obligations spending, and veterans' benefits.
Three-quarters of the interest on the national debt is
included, as well as an estimate of the fraction of that
debt which is war incurred.

12. For one thing, the space program is typically classified
as civilian although much of it is essentially military
in its character.

13. Richard Halloran, "Machinery, Manufactured Goods Replace Oil as the Top U.S. Import," New York Times
(July 5, 1978).

14. Kenneth A. Briggs, "Southern Baptists Call for Arms Limit," New York Times (June 15, 1978).

15. "Billy Graham: A Change of Heart," Sojourners (August 1979).

16. George Wald, "A Generation in Search of a Future," a speech delivered on March 4, 1969 at Kresge Auditorium of the Massachusetts Institute of Technology (Caedmon Records, New York). Reprinted in Fabrizio, R. Karas, E. and Menmuir, R. eds, The Rhetoric of No (New York: Holt, Rinehart and Winston, Inc., 1970).